HUMAN WORLD

COUNTRIES

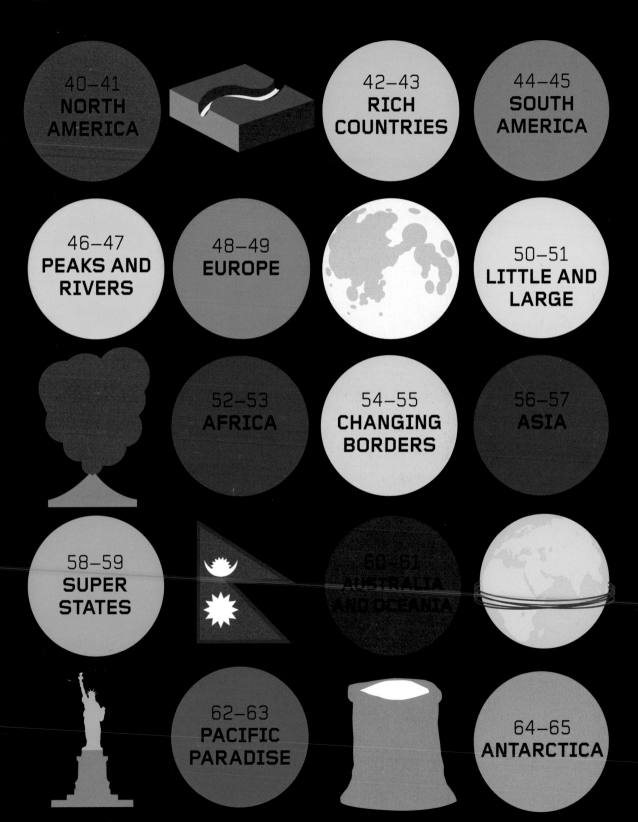

MACHINES AND VEHICLES

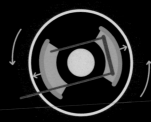

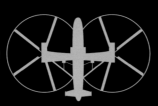

TECHNOLOGY

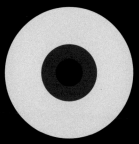

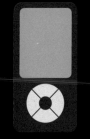
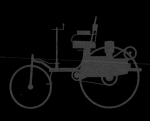

ART AND ENTERTAINMENT

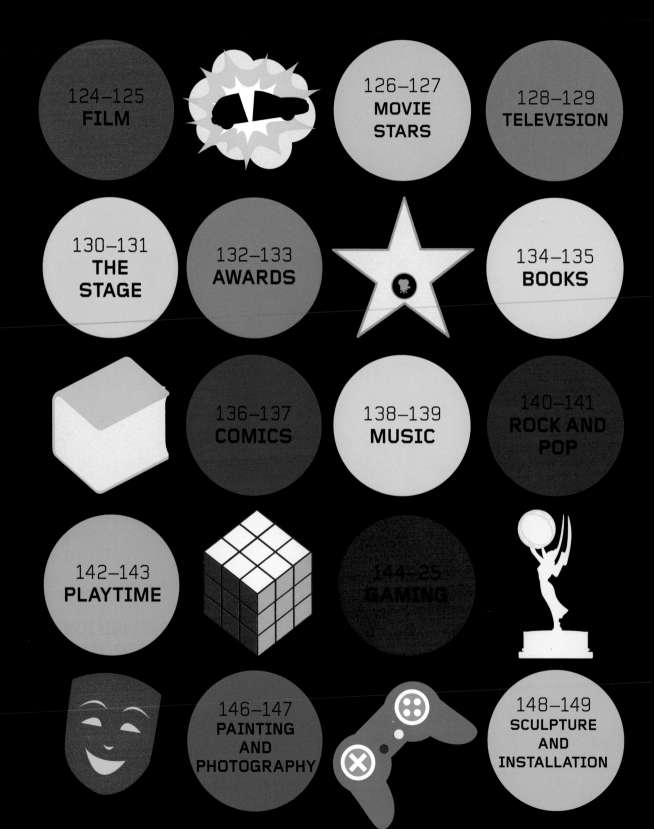

SPORT

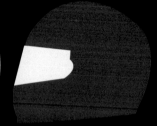
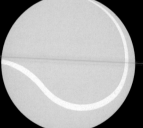

WELCOME TO THE WORLD OF INFOGRAPHICS

Using icons, graphics and pictograms, infographics visualise data and information in a whole new way!

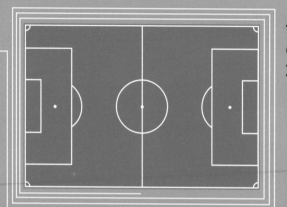

WRAP THE WORLD'S LONGEST COMIC STRIP AROUND A FOOTBALL PITCH.

FIND OUT HOW AN ENORMOUS OCEAN LINER CAN FLOAT.

SEE HOW A 3-D MOVIE LEAPS OFF THE SCREEN.

DISCOVER HOW THE WORLD LONG JUMP RECORD COMPARES TO A KANGAROO'S LEAP.

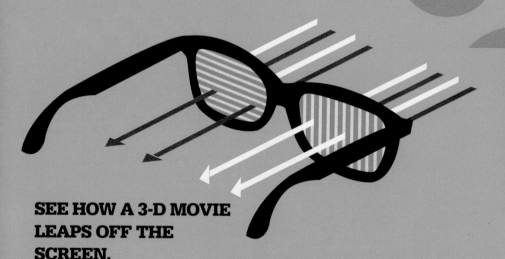

DISCOVER HOW MANY LEGO BRICKS IT TAKES TO CONNECT THE EARTH AND THE MOON.

FIND OUT HOW MANY MORE PENGUINS THAN PEOPLE THERE ARE IN ANTARCTICA.

PLACE THE WORLD'S TALLEST BUILDINGS SIDE-BY-SIDE.

COMPARE THE BIGGEST WAVE EVER SURFED TO THE HEIGHT OF A BUS.

SEE HOW MUCH FOOD IS THROWN AWAY EVERY SINGLE DAY.

MEASURE THE DEPTH OF THE GRAND CANYON USING THE STATUE OF LIBERTY.

MORE AND MORE PEOPLE

Improvements in diet and health care over the last 100 years have meant that many people are living for longer and fewer are dying young. This has led to an explosion in the world's population.

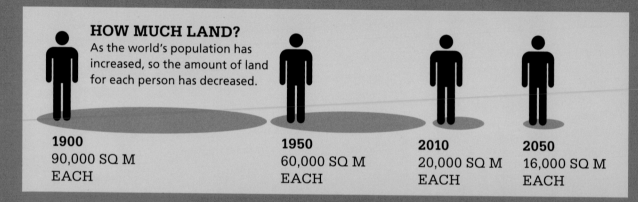

HOW MUCH LAND?
As the world's population has increased, so the amount of land for each person has decreased.

1900
90,000 SQ M
EACH

1950
60,000 SQ M
EACH

2010
20,000 SQ M
EACH

2050
16,000 SQ M
EACH

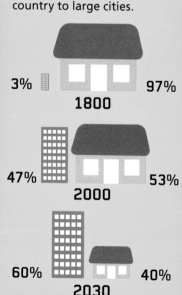

CITY VS COUNTRY
Since 1800, more and more people have moved from the country to large cities.

3% 97%
1800

47% 53%
2000

60% 40%
2030

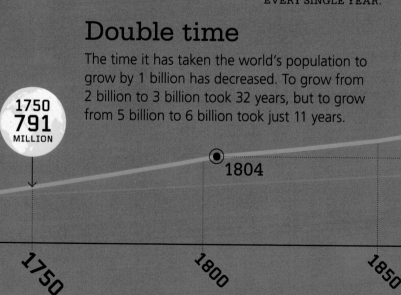

THE WORLD'S POPULATION IS INCREASING BY

74,000,000

EVERY SINGLE YEAR.

Double time

The time it has taken the world's population to grow by 1 billion has decreased. To grow from 2 billion to 3 billion took 32 years, but to grow from 5 billion to 6 billion took just 11 years.

1750
791
MILLION

1804

1750

1800

1850

108
BILLION
The number of people
who have ever lived.

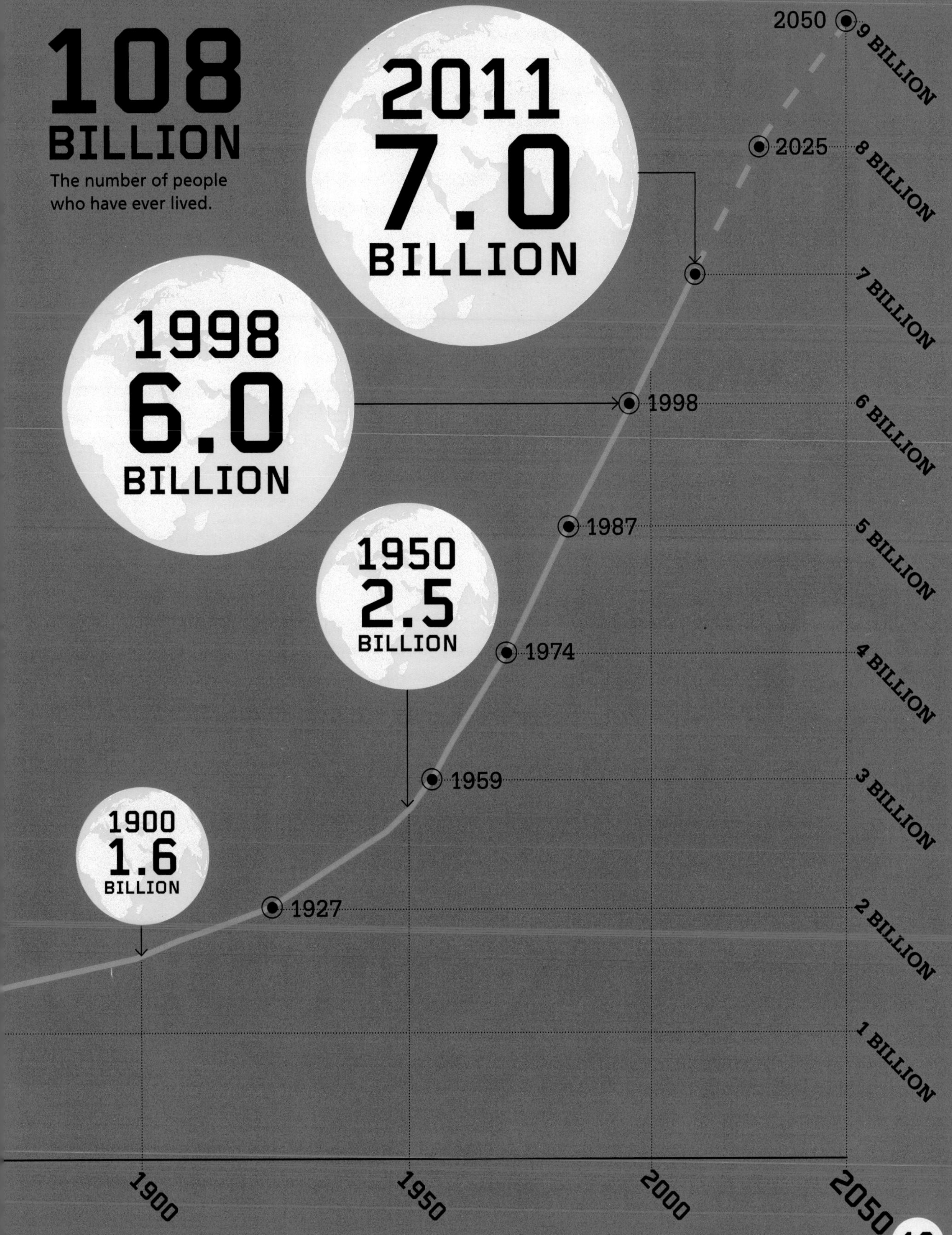

2011
7.0
BILLION

1998
6.0
BILLION

1950
2.5
BILLION

1900
1.6
BILLION

2050 ● 9 BILLION

● 2025   8 BILLION

● 7 BILLION

● 1998   6 BILLION

● 1987   5 BILLION

● 1974   4 BILLION

● 1959   3 BILLION

● 1927   2 BILLION

1 BILLION

1900

1950

2000

2050

WHERE IN THE WORLD?

The distribution of the world's population is very uneven. While in some areas the average space each person has is the area of a small room, in others it can be the size of a town.

EUROPE
POPULATION
732,759,000
10.61%
OF WORLD
POPULATION

GREENLAND
lowest population density in the world. Each person has 38.5 square kilometres.

NORTH AMERICA
POPULATION
351,659,000
5.09%
OF WORLD
POPULATION

67
Population of the country with the fewest people – the Pitcairn Islands in the middle of the Pacific Ocean.

LATIN AMERICA AND THE CARIBBEAN
POPULATION
588,649,000
8.52%
OF WORLD POPULATION...>

AFRICA
POPULATION
1,033,043,000
14.95%
OF WORLD
POPULATION

ASIA

POPULATION

4,166,741,000

60.31%

OF WORLD POPULATION

MACAU, CHINA
highest population density in the world. Each person has 0.00005 square kilometres.

1,336,720,000

Population of the People's Republic of China, the country with the most citizens.

OCEANIA
POPULATION
35,838,000
0.52%
OF WORLD POPULATION

The ten countries with the largest number of people account for 58.7 per cent of the world's population. The other countries – nearly 200 – have just 41.3%.

58.7%   **41.3%**

CITY LIVING

Towns and cities are found in nearly every part of the world, from mountain peaks to arid deserts. Some are so big, that more people live in them than in whole countries.

FIVE BIGGEST CITIES

The figures shown here represent the number of people found in each of these urban agglomerations. An agglomeration is a built-up area made up of the city and any suburbs that are linked to it.

2. DELHI
INDIA

22,157,000

Delhi is the largest agglomeration in terms of its area. Each person living here has an average space of 0.0015 square kilometres.

5. MEXICO CITY
MEXICO

19,460,000

Nine million people live in Mexico City, with the rest living in neighbouring areas.

3. SAO PAULO
BRAZIL

20,262,000

Covering an area of 8,000 sq km, Sao Paulo is the most populous city in the entire Americas.

4. MUMBAI
INDIA

20,041,000

Each person living in the agglomeration of Mumbai has an average of just 0.00006 square kilometres.

NORTHERNMOST AND SOUTHERNMOST SETTLEMENTS

The Canadian settlement of Alert lies just 817 km from the North Pole. At the other end of the Earth, Amundsen-Scott is a scientific base at the South Pole.

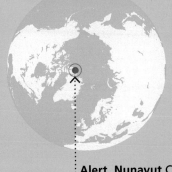

Amundsen-Scott base
South Pole

Alert, Nunavut Canada

LA RINCONADA ┈┈>
PERU 5,099 M

LA PAZ ┈┈>
BOLIVIA 3,640 M

CUZCO ┈┈>
PERU 3,300 M

HIGHEST AND LOWEST

The settlement of La Rinconada is close to a gold mine high up in the Andes Mountains. Despite its remote location, 30,000 people live and work there.

DENVER ┈┈>
USA 1,609 M

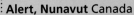

1. TOKYO
JAPAN
36,669,000

The Greater Tokyo Area is the largest agglomeration in the world. It is so big that it has swallowed other cities entirely, including Yokohama, which has 3 million people on its own.

In 1950, there were **83** cities with populations of more than **1 million** people. By **2007**, this had risen to **468**.

PARIS
FRANCE 35 METRES ┈┈>

SEA LEVEL

JERICHO, WEST BANK
APPROX 250 METRES ┈┈>
BELOW SEA LEVEL

17

REACH FOR THE SKY

Modern skyscrapers soar high into the air and are places where thousands of people live, work, shop and even relax in parks and swimming pools.

The height of the world's first skyscraper, the Home Insurance Building built in Chicago in 1885.

42 M

BURJ KHALIFA

The tallest building in the world contains:

160-ROOM HOTEL
11 HECTARES OF PARK
3,000 UNDERGROUND PARKING SPACES
26,000 PANES OF GLASS

The Great Pyramid of Giza in Egypt was the tallest building in the world from 2570 BCE until 1311 CE. It is made from approximately 2.3 million stone blocks and weighs about 5.75 million tonnes.

GREAT PYRAMID AT GIZA
147 M

TALLEST CITIES IN THE WORLD

These figures show the calculated average height of the ten tallest (CAHTT) buildings in each city. In 2010, Dubai became the world's tallest city when the Burj Khalifa was officially opened.

DUBAI
1,150.5

HONG KONG
1,080.9

CHICAGO
1,036.5

SHANGHAI
1,010.3

GUANGZHOU
945.7

NEW YORK CITY
940.8

BURJ KHALIFA, DUBAI, UNITED ARAB EMIRATES 829.84 M

CN TOWER, TORONTO, CANADA 553.33 M

WILLIS TOWER, CHICAGO, USA 527 M

TAIPEI 101, TAIPEI, TAIWAN 509.2 M

PETRONAS TOWERS, KUALA LUMPUR, MALAYSIA 451.9 M

The two Petronas Towers in Kuala Lumpur, Malaysia, are linked by a bridge at the 41st and 42nd floors.

EIFFEL TOWER, PARIS, FRANCE 324 M

2,500,000 The number of rivets used to build the Eiffel Tower.

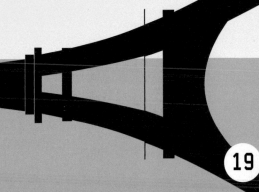

RICH WORLD, POOR WORLD

Trade spreads money and wealth around the world. But this wealth is not spread evenly – many people are very poor while some countries can afford to borrow enormous amounts of money.

WHERE ARE THE RICH?

This map shows the percentage of the world's wealth held by different areas around the globe.

NORTH AMERICA
28%

SOUTH AMERICA
4%

THE RICHEST 0.5% OF THE WORLD'S POPULATION OWN 38.5% OF ITS WEALTH THE POOREST TWO THIRDS OWN JUST 3.3%

World trade

Countries need to buy in certain goods from other parts of the world – this is called importing. The graphics below show the countries that import the most.

90%

The amount of the world's trade that is carried around the globe by shipping.

USA 2,314,000,000,000

CHINA 1,743,000,000,000

Import levels 2011 (US$).

US$1.7 TRILLION

The amount the public debt of the USA increased by in 2010. It rose by US$1.9 trillion in 2009 and US$1 trillion in 2008.

WHO OWES WHAT?

Countries may need to borrow money, for example in order to build hospitals or buy weapons for their armed forces. The money they borrow is called the public debt.

EUROPE 34%

CHINA 9%

ASIA PACIFIC 22%

INDIA 2%

AFRICA 1%

USA 13,471

JAPAN 12,352

 GERMANY 2,794

 ITALY 2,410

 CHINA 1,599

 INDIA 1,243

Public debt per country 2014 (US$ billions)

INDIA	CHINA	GERMANY	ITALY	USA	JAPAN
1,007	1,194	34,213	39,399	42,525	98,377

Public debt per person 2014 (US$).

GERMANY 1,198,000,000,000

JAPAN 794,700,000,000

GOING GLOBAL

Some of the world's biggest corporations earn more money each year than entire countries. These companies employ thousands, and sometimes millions of people around the globe.

EXXON MOBIL 385.65
OIL AND GAS PRODUCERS

APPLE 378.25
TECHNOLOGY HARDWARE, SOFTWARE AND EQUIPMENT

Big earners
The figures in this graphic compare the market value of the world's largest companies. This value is based on the total value of their shares as they are bought and sold at stock exchanges around the world.

GOOGLE 259.13
INTERNET-RELATED SERVICES AND PRODUCTS

WALMART 258.49
DISCOUNT DEPARTMENT STORES

MICROSOFT 241.45
SOFTWARE AND COMPUTER SERVICES

McDONALD'S
This burger chain sells more than

75

hamburgers every single second and serves about

62,000,000

people every day – that's greater than the population of the UK.

McDONALD'S IS FOUND IN

119

COUNTRIES.

World's largest companies, first quarter 2014 (US$ millions)

GLOBAL EXPOSURE

The figures below show the percentage of the world in which the most widespread companies operate, employ people and sell their goods and services.

XSTRATA	ABB LTD	NOKIA	EXXON	TOYOTA
Mining and quarrying 93.2%	Engineering Services 90.4%	Electrical and electronic equipment 90.3%	Oil and gas production 68%	Car maker 30.9%

WALMART
LARGEST PRIVATE EMPLOYER IN THE WORLD. IT HAS

8,500

STORES IN 15 COUNTRIES UNDER 55 DIFFERENT NAMES. THESE NAMES INCLUDE WAL-MART, ASDA, SEIYU AND BEST PRICE.

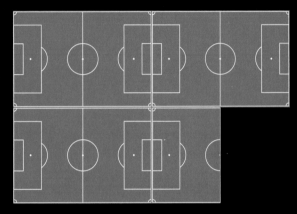

The largest Walmart store is in Albany, New York, USA. It covers 24,154.8 square metres – an area as large as 3.5 football pitches.

WALMART (USA)	CHINA NATIONAL PETROLEUM (CHINA)	STATE GRID (CHINA)	INDIAN RAILWAYS (INDIA)	SINOPEC (CHINA)
2,100,000 employees	1,649,992 employees	1,533,800 employees	1,361,519 employees	633,383 employees

WORLD'S BIGGEST EMPLOYERS 2011 (NOT INCLUDING NON-CORPORATE PUBLIC EMPLOYERS)

WATER

Without water, life would not be possible. But not everyone has access to safe water, while other people can pour thousands of litres of water down the drain every year.

OF ALL THE WORLD'S WATER...

Access to water

Processing water so that it is safe to drink is expensive and many countries cannot afford to supply their population with safe water. According to the World Health Organisation, 884 million people do not have access to a safe water supply – that is nearly three times the population of the USA.

FRESHWATER
2.5%

OF THAT, ONLY
30%
is usable water, the remainder of the freshwater is locked in glaciers.

50 billion bottles of water are bought in the USA every year, creating **US$30 billion** in sales.

According to the UN, this amount of money would be enough to provide everyone on the planet with access to safe water.

WHO USES THE MOST?
water per person per day, in litres.

USA **575**

AUSTRALIA **493**

ITALY **386**

JAPAN **374**

Water usage

A person taking a five-minute shower in a developed country, such as the USA, will use more than 50 litres of water. That is more than a person in a developing country will use in an entire day.

WHO USES THE LEAST?
water per person per day (in litres)

HAITI **15**   RWANDA **15**   UGANDA **15**   MOZAMBIQUE **5**

1 CUP OF COFFEE
140 LITRES

WATER FOOTPRINT
Water is used to produce all the food we eat. But some foods require a lot more processing and so use a lot more water in their production.

1 KG OF CHOCOLATE
24,000 LITRES

1 KG OF BEEF
15,500 LITRES

1 SLICE OF BREAD
40 LITRES

WHAT A WASTE!

Humans are very wasteful and throw away millions of tonnes of useful food and materials every year. With more careful use, everyone on the planet could be fed with what's discarded.

Where does it go?

The vast amount of material thrown away each year could be recycled and used again. However, most of it is used only once and then discarded in landfill or burned in incinerators.

TRASH TREATMENT AROUND THE WORLD

54% LANDFILL

24% RECYCLED

12% INCINERATED

8% COMPOSTED

 84% COULD BE RECYCLED

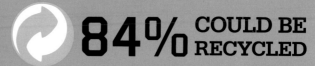

NEW YORK CITY PRODUCES 11,000 TONNES OF TRASH A DAY.
In our lifetime, 307 million Americans will produce 280 billion cubic metres of rubbish – enough to cover

Only **20%** of plastic bottles are recycled out of **29.8 billion**. Recycling the other **80%** could earn **US$1.2 billion**, based on a price of 5 cents per bottle.

THE CITY OF GUIYU IN CHINA IS THE CENTRE OF A HUGE ELECTRONICS RECYCLING INDUSTRY. EACH YEAR,

5,500

COMPANIES IN THE CITY EMPLOY ABOUT

150,000

PEOPLE TO DISMANTLE COMPUTERS, MOBILE PHONES AND OTHER ELECTRONIC DEVICES.

70%

It takes 70 per cent less energy to make recycled paper than to make paper from raw materials.

1974
900 CALORIES OF FOOD WASTED PER PERSON PER DAY

TODAY
1,400 CALORIES OF FOOD WASTED PER PERSON PER DAY

2,000,000,000

people could be fed with the amount of food the USA throws away each year.

8,300,000

tonnes of food are wasted in the UK every year.

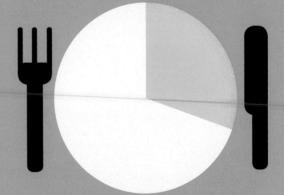

30.8% OF ALL FOOD PURCHASED IN THE UK IS THROWN AWAY.

DWINDLING RESOURCES

Humans take resources out of the ground and use them in nearly everything that's manufactured. However, the speed with which we are using these resources means that many of them will run out very soon.

GLOBAL OIL CONSUMPTION =
30.6 BILLION
BARRELS PER YEAR

OIL RESERVES =
1.3 TRILLION
BARRELS

OIL WILL
RUN OUT IN
2053

USA **19,150,000**

CHINA **9,189,000**

JAPAN
4,452,000

INDIA
3,182,000

RUSSIA
2,937,000

ISLAND OF NIUE 40

OIL – WHO USES THE MOST?
(barrels per day)

Using resources

Everything you use, whether it is a car, a mobile phone or a watch, needs resources to make it. We also use resources to power our homes, factories and work places.

THE RICHEST 20% OF PEOPLE CONSUME 83% OF RESOURCES.

THE POOREST 20% OF PEOPLE CONSUME 1.3% OF RESOURCES.

430

The number of nuclear reactors around the world at the start of 2014.

PHOSPHORUS (FERTILISER, ANIMAL FEED) 345 YEARS

TANTALUM (MOBILE PHONES, CAMERA LENSES) 116 YEARS

NICKEL (BATTERIES, TURBINE BLADES) 90 YEARS

URANIUM (WEAPONS, POWER STATIONS) 59 YEARS

COPPER (WIRE, COINS, PLUMBING) 61 YEARS

GOLD (JEWELLERY, DENTAL) 45 YEARS

LEAD (PIPES, BATTERIES) 42 YEARS

TIN (CANS, SOLDER) 40 YEARS

OTHER RESOURCES – WHEN WILL THEY GO?
Years remaining of mineral reserves

COAL PROVIDES NEARLY **30%** OF THE WORLD'S ENERGY NEEDS, INCLUDING POWER AND HEATING

AND IS USED TO GENERATE MORE THAN **40%** OF THE WORLD'S ELECTRICITY.

GETTING ABOUT

Today, nearly every person on the planet has access to some form of transport, whether this is a car for short journeys or a passenger jet to fly around the world. However, this increase in travelling has a huge impact on the environment.

CAR PRODUCTION

In 2013, 65,433,287 cars were built around the world. The biggest manufacturers were:

CHINA
18,085,213

JAPAN
8,189,323

THERE ARE APPROXIMATELY

600,000,000

PASSENGER CARS IN THE WORLD TODAY. THAT IS ONE FOR EVERY 11 PEOPLE.

GERMANY
5,439,904

USA
4,346,958

Car world

The most popular car model is the Toyota Corolla. Since it was first sold in 1966, 32 million have been produced around the world.

SOUTH KOREA
4,122,604

INDIA
3,138,988

BRAZIL
2,742,309

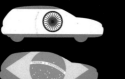

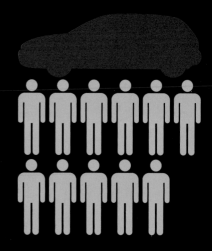

5.8%
NON-ROAD TRANSPORT

4%
R NON-
SPORT

1
CO
FOR

5.9%
TRANSPORT

43.9%
ELECTRICITY GENERATION

18.2%
MANUFACTURING
AND CONSTRUCTION

MISSIONS
oxide (CO_2) plays a major part in climate change.
ures show the main sources of CO_2 emissions.

RNATIONAL TRAVEL
of international tourists worldwide

1950
MILLION

1970
105.8 MILLION

1990
439.5 MILLION

2010
1.05 BILL

WORLD'S BUSIEST AIRPORTS
The busiest airports in the world with the numbers
of passengers they handle each year.

ANTA, USA
3 032 086

HEATHROW, UK
66 037 578

BEIJING, CHINA
65 372 012

CHICAGO, USA
64 158 343

TOKYO, JA
61 903 6

WORK, REST AND PLAY

As more and more people travel around the world on holiday, the amount of money they bring into other countries can have a huge effect on local economies.

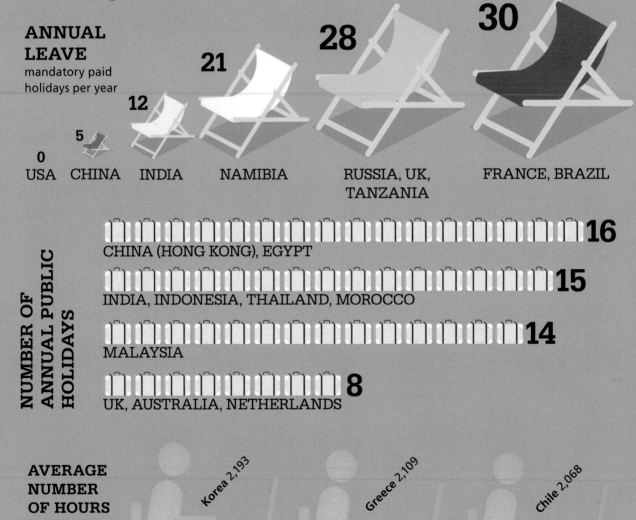

ANNUAL LEAVE
mandatory paid holidays per year

0 — USA
5 — CHINA
12 — INDIA
21 — NAMIBIA
28 — RUSSIA, UK, TANZANIA
30 — FRANCE, BRAZIL

NUMBER OF ANNUAL PUBLIC HOLIDAYS

16 — CHINA (HONG KONG), EGYPT
15 — INDIA, INDONESIA, THAILAND, MOROCCO
14 — MALAYSIA
8 — UK, AUSTRALIA, NETHERLANDS

AVERAGE NUMBER OF HOURS WORKED PER YEAR

Korea 2,193
Greece 2,109
Chile 2,068

MOST POPULAR TOURIST COUNTRIES
International tourist arrivals

France 76.8 million

USA 59.7 million

China 55.7 million

Spain 52.7 million

Italy 43.6 million

UK 28.1 million

IN 2013, INCOME FROM INTERNATIONAL TOURISM GREW TO **US$1.4 TRILLION** – THAT IS MORE THAN THE ENTIRE COUNTRY OF TURKEY EARNS IN A YEAR.

TOURISM INCOME
Top three biggest earners from the tourist industry (US$ billions)

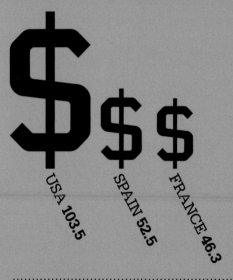

USA 103.5

SPAIN 52.5

FRANCE 46.3

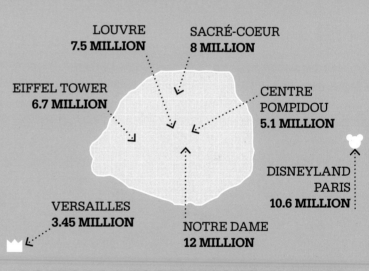

LOUVRE
7.5 MILLION

SACRÉ-COEUR
8 MILLION

EIFFEL TOWER
6.7 MILLION

CENTRE POMPIDOU
5.1 MILLION

DISNEYLAND PARIS
10.6 MILLION

VERSAILLES
3.45 MILLION

NOTRE DAME
12 MILLION

POPULAR DESTINATIONS IN PARIS
Number of visitors to attractions in the world's most popular tourist city

USA 1,778

Japan 1,733

UK 1,647

France 1,554

Netherlands 1,377

STAYING IN TOUCH

The first writing appeared more than 5,000 years ago. Since then, many amazing inventions have greatly changed the way we communicate, allowing us to send messages around the globe in the blink of an eye.

THE INTERNET
The number of people using various languages on the internet.

ENGLISH
536,000,000

CHINESE
509,000,000

SPANISH
164,000,000

Languages
There are thought to be up to 7,000 different languages spoken around the world.

MANDARIN CHINESE **12.44%**

SPANISH **4.85%**

ENGLISH **4.83%**

ARABIC **3.25%**

HINDI **2.68%**

THE REST **71.95%**

THE SPOKEN WORD
Most popular first languages as a percentage of the world's population.

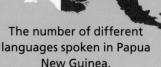

832

The number of different languages spoken in Papua New Guinea.

TALKING LONG-DISTANCE

Key moments in the history of
long-distance communication

HUMAN RUNNER
In 490 BCE, Pheidippides ran
225 km from Athens to Sparta
in two days, with news of the
Battle of Marathon.

SEMAPHORE TOWERS
The arms on these towers
moved to spell out messages.
They were used throughout
western Europe by Napoleon
in the early 19th century.

MORSE CODE
Using dots and dashes, the
first morse code signal was
sent on 6 January 1838.

PONY EXPRESS
This delivery service reduced
message delivery time across
the whole of the USA from
several weeks to just 10 days.

AIRMAIL
The first official air mail
delivery was on 17 August
1859. John Wise piloted a
balloon from Lafayette,
Indiana, to New York.

TELEPHONE
The first call was made by
Alexander Graham Bell on
10 March 1876.

WIRELESS
The first transatlantic radio
message was sent in 1901.

MOBILE PHONE
The first call from a mobile
phone was made on the
3 April 1973.

In 2010, there were some
5.3 billion mobile phones in
use. The countries with the greatest number
were China with **747,000,000** and
India with **670,000,000** users.

GOING POSTAL
300,000,000,000
letters are posted each year around the world.

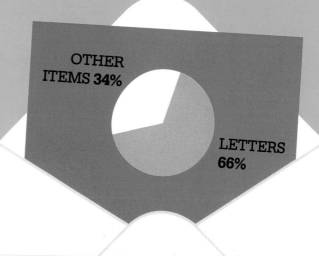

OTHER ITEMS 34%

LETTERS 66%

PROPORTION OF ITEMS POSTED EACH YEAR

5,500,000,000
letters are sent internationally.

4,000,000,000
of these are carried by plane.

THE DIGITAL WORLD

The first email was sent in 1971. Today, we type and send nearly 400 times as many emails as we do written letters.

RISE OF THE COMPUTERS

The number of computers has more than doubled since the start of the 21st century.

2000 **140.2 MILLION**

2010 **350.9 MILLION**

EMAIL

There are **3,150,000,000** known email accounts in the world. **25%** of these are company accounts.

In 2011, there were **2,110,000,000** internet users around the world. China had **485,000,000** while the US had **245,000,000**.

THE WORLD'S FIRST PROGRAMMABLE, FULLY AUTOMATIC COMPUTING MACHINE WAS THE ZUSE Z3, BUILT IN 1941.

BY THE END OF 2011, THERE WERE **555,000,000** WEBSITES, OF WHICH SOME **300,000,000** HAD BEEN CREATED THAT YEAR ALONE.

107,000,000,000,000

EMAILS WERE SENT IN 2010

OF WHICH

89%

WERE SPAM
RELATED.

You Tube™

35 HOURS

of video are uploaded to
YouTube every minute.

KEEP TAKING THE TABLETS

How the type of computer we use will change worldwide:

2008
FIGURES

2015
PROJECTIONS

DESKTOP

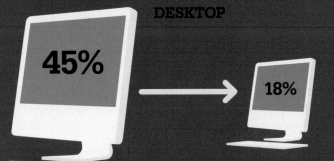

45% → 18%

f

1.23 BILLION

people were using Facebook by the
end of 2013. More than 200 million
of these signed up in that year.

350 MILLION

photos are uploaded to
Facebook every day.

LAPTOP

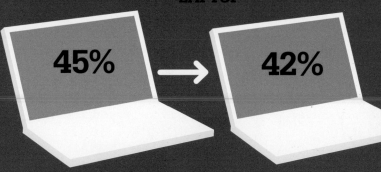

45% → **42%**

NETBOOK/MINI PC

9% → 17%

500,000,000

tweets are sent on average
every day.

TABLET

1% → **23%**

NORTH AMERICA

Stretching from the Arctic to the Caribbean, North America covers 24 million square kilometres, making up about 16 per cent of the world's land area.

HIGHEST POINT ON THE CONTINENT
Mt McKinley (Alaska, USA)

6,194 m

Mount McKinley

Canada has the world's longest coastline, measuring

202,080 KM

... enough to stretch around the world five times.

How a canyon forms

1. Fast-flowing water lifts rocks and mud out of the river bed, creating a channel.

2. As more debris is removed, this channel gets deeper. Over time, it may become deep enough to form a steep-sided canyon.

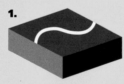

GRAND CANYON (ARIZONA, USA)
The world's largest land gorge ranges in width from

180 METRES TO 29 KM

Colorado River

Before the building of the Glen Canyon Dam, the Colorado River, which cut the Grand Canyon, could carry

500,000 TONNES

of rocks, mud and debris away every single day. This is the equivalent to the weight of more than four CN Towers – North America's tallest building.

THE GREAT LAKES

The five Great Lakes in Canada and the USA contain about **23,000 cubic km** of water. That is...

21%
of the world's surface freshwater

84%
of North America's freshwater supply

Lake Superior
Lake Huron
Lake Ontario
Lake Michigan
Lake Erie

<.... Mississippi River

Mississippi flow rate
At New Orleans, Louisiana, it is about **16,200** cubic metres **per second...**
... enough to fill **6.5 Olympic swimming pools**
every second.

LOWEST POINT ON THE CONTINENT
Death Valley (California, USA)
86 m below sea level.

THE GRAND CANYON IS UP TO 1,800 M DEEP – MORE THAN 19 TIMES THE STATUE OF LIBERTY.

RICH COUNTRIES

Much of North America is made up of three large countries – the USA, Canada and Mexico. It also includes Greenland, the world's largest island.

GREENLAND

Alaska

CANADA

UNITED STATES OF AMERICA

MEXICO

Hawaii

The border between Canada and the USA is the world's longest land border, measuring

8,893 km

(including 2,477 km with Alaska).

GDP PER PERSON

D.R. OF CONGO	MEXICO	GREENLAND	USA	CANADA	MONACO
US$231	US$10,047	US$22,508	US$48,112	US$50,345	US$172,676

THE WORLD'S TWO **RICHEST PEOPLE** ARE FROM NORTH AMERICA:

Carlos Slim (Mexico)
US$73 billion

Bill Gates (USA)
US$67 billion

THE USA IS A MAJOR FARMING NATION WITH **18%** OF ITS LAND GIVEN OVER TO CROPS, COMPARED TO **12.7%** IN MEXICO, **4.6%** IN CANADA AND LESS THAN **1%** IN GREENLAND.

4,760,000

THE NUMBER OF **TRACTORS** IN THE USA – MORE THAN ANY OTHER COUNTRY.

16
PER 1,000 PEOPLE

CANADA HAS 732,600

23
PER 1,000 PEOPLE

PRISONERS
Numbers per 100,000 people

715

116

US WEALTH
Gross National Income
(highest in the world)

US$9,780,000,000,000

BUT THIS WEALTH IS NOT EVENLY DISTRIBUTED

Poorest 10%

1.8%
share of income

Wealthiest 10%

30.5%
share of income

LIFE EXPECTANCY
average for
North America

MEN **73** YEARS

WOMEN **79** YEARS

SOUTH AMERICA

A large part of South America is covered by rainforest. The rainforest around the Amazon River covers more than a third of the continent, or 6 million square kilometres.

The Amazon is the world's second **longest** river, but by far the **largest** by volume. It contains **20%** of all the world's river water.

Atlantic Ocean

Manaus

Amazon River

At its narrowest point in **Panama**, Central America is just **50 km wide.** The mouth of the Amazon is **320 km wide.**

SOUTH AMERICA

205,000 L

Every second, **205,000** cubic metres of water pour out of the Amazon into the Atlantic Ocean.

That is **5 times** more than the world's next largest river, the Congo, and **60 times** more than the longest river, the Nile.

Near Manaus, Brazil, an area of rainforest covering just **175 square metres** (about one-third the area of a football pitch), was found to contain...

1,652 plants belonging to **107 species** from **37 families.**

HIGHEST LAKE IN THE WORLD

Lake Titcaca (on the border between Peru and Bolivia)

3,810 m above sea level.

Lake Titcaca

Iquitos

Atacama Desert

IQUITOS (PERU)

274 cm per year

ATACAMA DESERT (CHILE)

0.01 cm per year

Average rainfall

RAINFOREST LAYERS

Plants in a rainforest grow to different heights, creating various layers, from the emergents down to the forest floor.

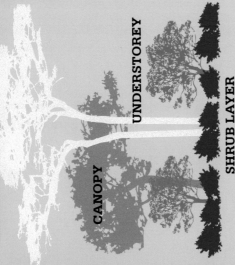

EMERGENT LAYER

CANOPY

UNDERSTOREY

SHRUB LAYER

RAINFALL

The Atacama Desert in Chile is one of the driest places on Earth.

Some areas have had no rainfall for more than **400 YEARS.**

50% The amount that glaciers have shrunk in the Andes due to global warming.

PEAKS AND RIVERS

About 80% of Chile is covered with mountains.

Chile is more than **4,000 km long,** but is only **150 km** wide on average.

The countries of South America cover about one-eighth of the world's land area. These nations include thousands of tiny islands scattered about the Caribbean Sea.

Brazil takes up 47.8 per cent of South America.

La Paz, Bolivia, is the highest capital city in the world, at an altitude of **3,600 metres.**

Brazil has a population of **199,321,413**

It is the fifth most populous country in the world, after China, India, the USA and Indonesia.

GUATEMALA

THE BAHAMAS

CUBA

HAITI

PUERTO RICO

ST KITTS AND NEVIS

ANTIGUA AND BARBUDA

DOMINICA

ST VINCENT AND THE GRENADINES

BARBADOS

TRINIDAD AND TOBAGO

DOMINICAN REPUBLIC

ST LUCIA

GRENADA

JAMAICA

BELIZE

HONDURAS

PANAMA

COSTA RICA

NICARAGUA

EL SALVADOR

ECUADOR

COLUMBIA

VENEZUELA

GUYANA

SURINAME

FRENCH GUIANA

BRAZIL

PERU

BOLIVIA

CHILE

PARAGUAY

ARGENTINA

URUGUAY

Bolivia has a navy with about 4,500 personnel – but it is a landlocked country with no direct access to the sea.

The dam used 12.3 million cubic metres of concrete and enough iron and steel to build **380 Eiffel Towers.**

←— Itaipú Dam is **196 m** high. —→

EIFFEL TOWER, PARIS, FRANCE
324 M

94%

Paraguay

20%

Brazil

That is enough to meet 20 per cent of Brazil's electricity needs AND 94 per cent of Paraguay's.

87%

Today, that figure is **87 per cent.**

The hydroelectric dam at Itaipú on the border between Brazil and Paraguay can generate more than **90,000 gigawatt hours per year.**

15%

In 1940, about **15 per cent** of Brazil's population lived in towns and cities.

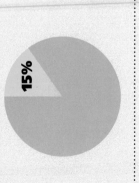

BRAZIL

Itaipú Dam

PARAGUAY

EUROPE

Europe is the world's second smallest continent. It stretches from the polar waters of the Arctic in the north to the warm Mediterranean Sea in the south.

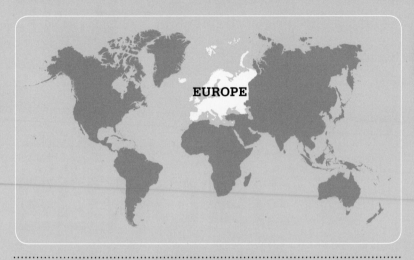

EUROPE

MOUNT ETNA

Standing **3,320 m** tall, Etna is Europe's highest active volcano. It measures about **150 km** around its base and covers **1,600 sq km**. That is about **15 per cent** of the island of Sicily, where it is located.

ICELAND

Iceland sits on the boundary between two of the Earth's tectonic plates (see page 49). As these plates move, red-hot liquid rock pours out, creating volcanoes.

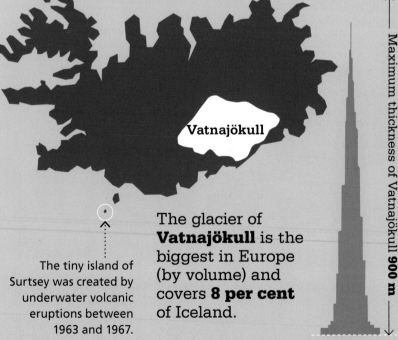

Vatnajökull

The tiny island of Surtsey was created by underwater volcanic eruptions between 1963 and 1967.

The glacier of **Vatnajökull** is the biggest in Europe (by volume) and covers **8 per cent** of Iceland.

Maximum thickness of Vatnajökull **900 m**

BURJ KHALIFA (Dubai) 829.84 M

LOWEST POINT
Caspian Sea shore (Russia)
28 m below sea level

HIGHEST POINT
Elbrus (Russia)
5,642 m

48

TECTONIC PLATES

The surface of the Earth is split up into massive plates of rock, called tectonic plates, which move about on the liquid rock beneath. Europe sits on the Eurasian Plate. The place where two plates meet is called a boundary.

TRANSFORM BOUNDARY

Two plates rub against each other – there are no transform boundaries in Europe.

DIVERGENT BOUNDARY

Two plates pull apart from each other, as is happening beneath Iceland between the Eurasian Plate and the North American Plate.

CONVERGENT BOUNDARY

Two plates crash into each other, as is happening between the Eurasian Plate and the African Plate.

The coastline of Norway is 100,915 km long, including fjords, indentations and islands.

UNINHABITED

INHABITED

GREECE CONTAINS MORE THAN

2,000 ISLANDS.

LESS THAN

9% OF THESE ARE INHABITED.

That is enough to stretch 2.5 times around the world.

LONGEST RIVER

The longest river in Europe is the Volga. It flows through western Russia for 3,530 km before emptying into the Caspian Sea. Altogether, the river system consists of 151,000 rivers and streams with a total length of

570,000 KM.

The distance to the Moon is 384,400 km.

Volga River

Black Sea *Caspian Sea*

LITTLE AND LARGE

Some of the richest countries in the world are found in Europe. Many Europeans can expect to live for a long time thanks to good health care and a high standard of living.

The tiny republic of San Marino attracts 3.5 million tourists every year.

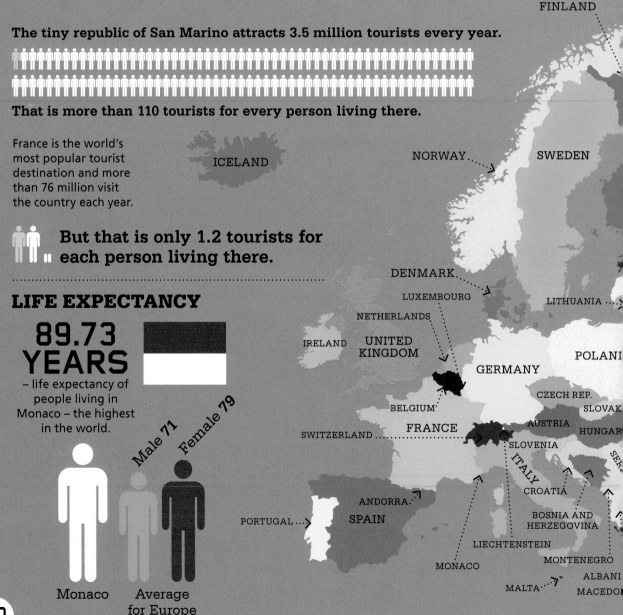

That is more than 110 tourists for every person living there.

France is the world's most popular tourist destination and more than 76 million visit the country each year.

But that is only 1.2 tourists for each person living there.

LIFE EXPECTANCY

89.73 YEARS

– life expectancy of people living in Monaco – the highest in the world.

Male 71   Female 79

Monaco   Average for Europe

FINLAND

ICELAND

NORWAY

SWEDEN

DENMARK

LUXEMBOURG

LITHUANIA

NETHERLANDS

IRELAND

UNITED KINGDOM

POLAND

GERMANY

CZECH REP.

SLOVAK

BELGIUM

AUSTRIA

HUNGAR

FRANCE

SWITZERLAND

SLOVENIA

SER

ITALY

CROATIA

PORTUGAL

ANDORRA

SPAIN

BOSNIA AND HERZEGOVINA

LIECHTENSTEIN

MONACO

MONTENEGRO

MALTA

ALBANI

MACEDO

HOT BEVERAGES

COFFEE

10.7 KG

0.7 KG

People in Ireland consume just 0.7 kg of coffee beans each year, while those in Norway consume 15 times more.

TEA

People in the UK consume 2.3 kg of tea leaves each year – 23 times as much as those who live in Italy.

2.3 KG

0.1 KG

Largest countries by population

Europe contains just 10 per cent of the world's population.

Russia	Germany	France	UK
143 MILLION	82 MILLION	63.5 MILLION	63 MILLION

EUROPEAN UNION

Twenty-eight of the continent's countries have formed a political and economic alliance called the European Union (EU). The Union is the world's biggest importer and exporter of goods.

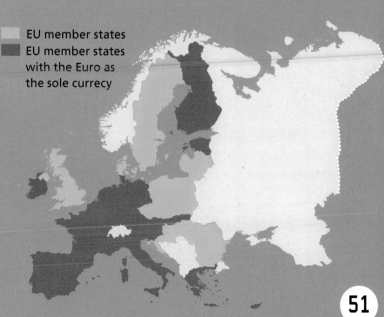

IMPORTS

EU $2.4 TRILLION   USA $2.35 TRILLION   China $1.8 TRILLION

EXPORTS

EU $2.2 TRILLION   China $2 TRILLION   USA $1.6 TRILLION

EU member states

EU member states with the Euro as the sole currecy

RUSSIA

..ESTONIA
....LATVIA

UKRAINE
····MOLDOVA

····ROMANIA
···BULGARIA
··TURKEY
GREECE

CYPRUS

51

AFRICA

Africa is a continent of contrasts, where mighty rivers flow through barren deserts and where frozen glaciers sit on the scorching Equator.

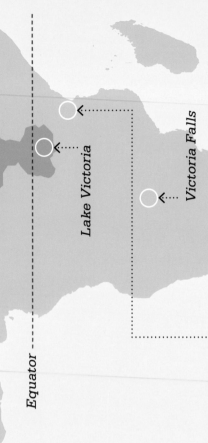

THE EQUATOR

The Equator runs through seven African countries – more than on any other continent and half the world's equatorial countries.

LOWEST POINT
Lake Assal (Djibouti)
155 m below sea level

Nile Basin

Lake Victoria

Victoria Falls

Equator

Conakry

HIGHEST POINT
Kilimanjaro (Tanzania)
5,898 m

AFRICA

Conakry, the capital city of Guinea is one of the wettest in Africa, with

3.7 metres of rain a year,

while Wadi Halfa, Sudan, is one of the driest, with just 3–5 mm.

THE NILE

The Nile is the world's longest river. It is

6,650 km
in length.

Its river basin covers about 10% of the continent.

10%

Nile River

LARGEST LAKE

Africa's largest lake is Lake Victoria on the borders of Uganda, Kenya and Tanzania. It covers

69,484 SQ KM

Lake Victoria

Victoria Falls

LARGEST WATERFALL

Victoria Falls is Africa's largest waterfall. On average, some 1,088 cubic metres of water flow over the falls each second – which could fill Wembley Stadium (UK) in **an hour.**

WEMBLEY STADIUM

NETHERLANDS

BELGIUM

FRANCE

Over the last 50 years, the Sahara has increased in size by **650,000 sq km** – larger than France, Belgium and the Netherlands combined.

Causes of desertification in Africa

5.8% Deforestation

57.8% Overgrazing

19.5% Agricultural activities

16.9% Overexploitation of vegetation for domestic use

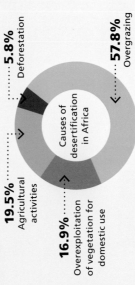

HOW DESERTS FORM

The transformation of fertile land into desert – known as desertification – happens in a number of ways. These include overgrazing by farm animals, cutting down forest, poor farming practices and the overuse of plants for home use, such as fuel.

The Sahara Desert covers about

8,600,000 sq km

which is about 28 per cent of the entire continent. It is also **bigger than Australia.**

Sahara

Australia

CHANGING BORDERS

The African continent contains more than 50 countries. The exact number frequently changes as some areas are disputed by two or more countries, while new countries emerge from civil wars.

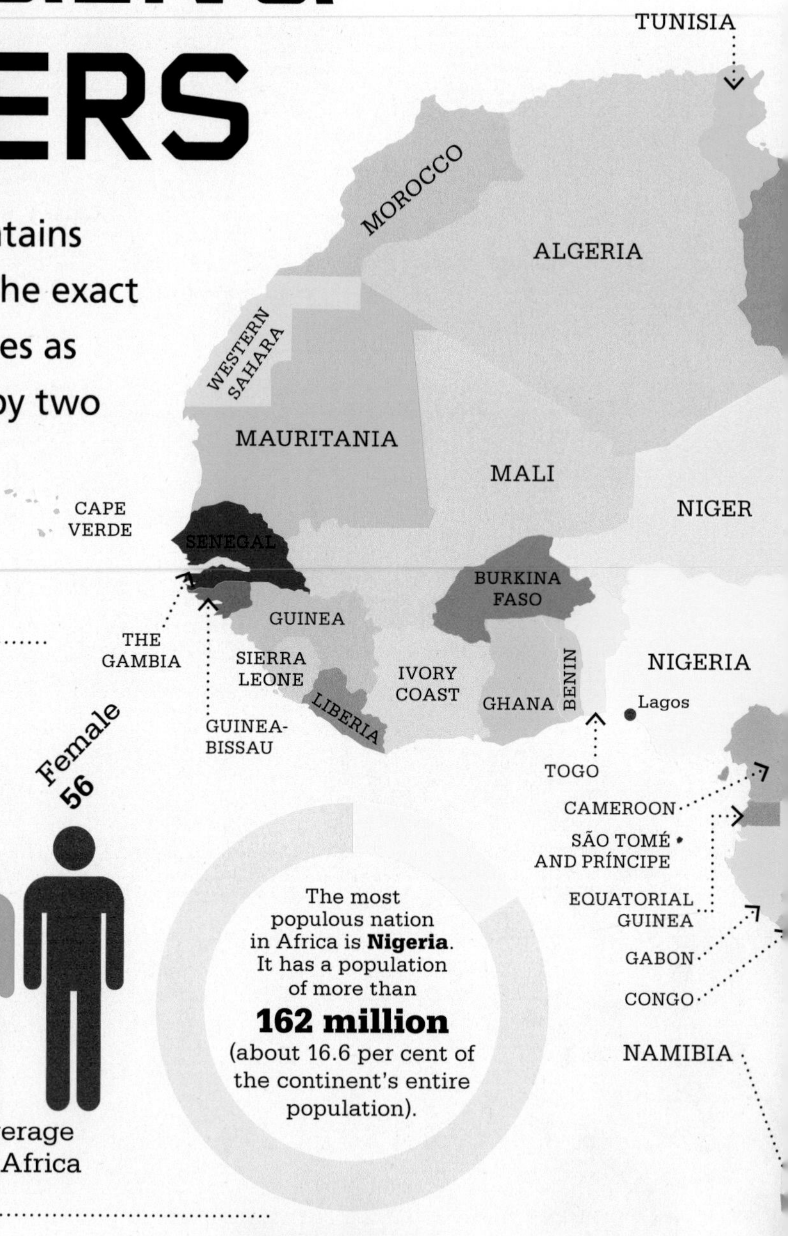
TUNISIA
MOROCCO
ALGERIA
WESTERN SAHARA
MAURITANIA
MALI
NIGER
CAPE VERDE
SENEGAL
BURKINA FASO
GUINEA
THE GAMBIA
SIERRA LEONE
IVORY COAST
GHANA
BENIN
NIGERIA
Lagos
LIBERIA
GUINEA-BISSAU
TOGO
CAMEROON
SÃO TOMÉ AND PRÍNCIPE
EQUATORIAL GUINEA
GABON
CONGO
NAMIBIA

LIFE EXPECTANCY

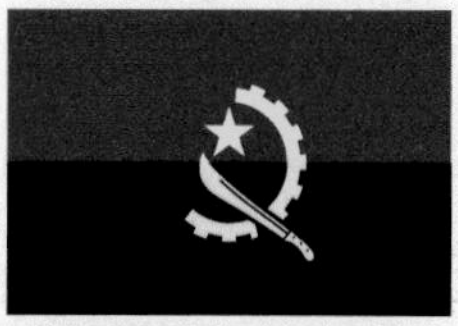

38.76 YEARS

the life expectancy of people living in Angola – the lowest in the world.

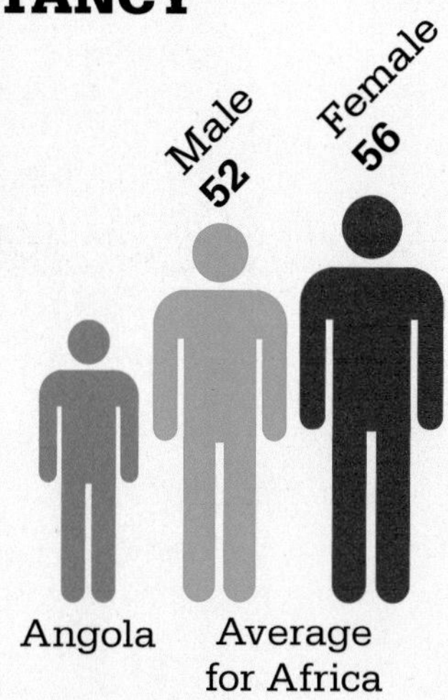
Male
52
Female
56
Angola
Average for Africa

The most populous nation in Africa is **Nigeria**. It has a population of more than

162 million

(about 16.6 per cent of the continent's entire population).

YOUNGEST COUNTRY IN THE WORLD

South Sudan
Declared a sovereign state on

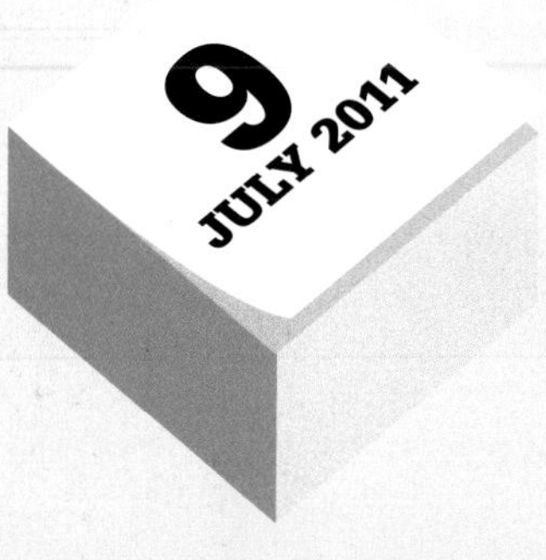
9
JULY 2011

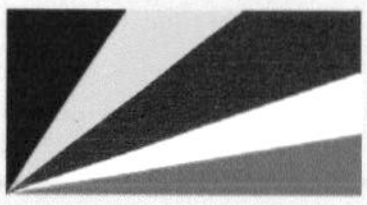

The Seychelles is Africa's smallest country. It is made up of 115 islands in the Indian Ocean. These have a total area of 455 sq km (about 2.5 times the size of Washington, DC), and a population of

90,000.

95%

of Egypt's population live along the banks of the Nile...

... in just **5 per cent** of the country's area.

95%

The Nile Valley is one of the world's most densely populated areas, with **1,540 people per sq km.**

Nile River

Cairo

LIBYA

EGYPT

Cairo

CHAD

SUDAN

ERITREA

DJIBOUTI

ETHIOPIA

CENTRAL
AFRICAN
REPUBLIC

SOUTH
SUDAN

SOMALIA

DEMOCRATIC
REPUBLIC OF
THE CONGO

UGANDA

KENYA

inshasa

RWANDA

BURUNDI

TANZANIA

SEYCHELLES

ANGOLA

ZAMBIA

MALAWI

MOZAMBIQUE

COMOROS

MADAGASCAR

ZIMBABWE

BOTSWANA

LESOTHO

SOUTH
AFRICA

SWAZILAND

Biggest cities

The Egyptian capital of **Cairo** is Africa's largest city with a population of

11 million.

Lagos, Nigeria

10.6 million

Kinshasa, D.R. of Congo

8.75 million

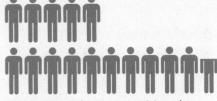

As more people move to cities, they will grow in size. Kinshasa will have a population of

15.8 million
by 2020.

ASIA

The world's largest continent stretches from the Mediterranean in the west to the Pacific in the east. It is filled with enormous forests, huge grassy plains and the planet's highest peaks.

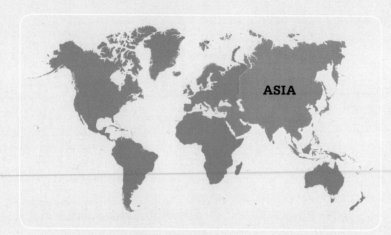

ASIA

CHINA is the biggest country in Asia. It covers 9,572,900 sq km...

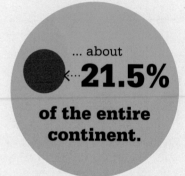

... about **21.5%** of the entire continent.

Asia (including the Asian part of Russia) makes up about one-third of the planet's land surface. That is

44,614,000 SQ KM

DECLINE OF THE ARAL SEA

Aral Sea

HIGHEST AND LOWEST POINTS IN ASIA

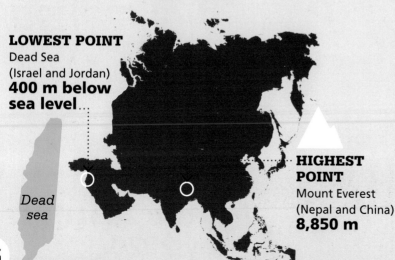

LOWEST POINT
Dead Sea
(Israel and Jordan)
400 m below sea level

Dead sea

HIGHEST POINT
Mount Everest
(Nepal and China)
8,850 m

1957   **2000**

The diversion of the rivers that used to feed the Aral Sea have caused it to shrink. At the current rate, it will disappear completely by 2020.

20-25 MILLION YEARS
The age of Lake Baikal, Russia, the world's oldest freshwater lake.

Lake Baikal is the largest freshwater lake by volume and holds 20 per cent of the Earth's surface freshwater.

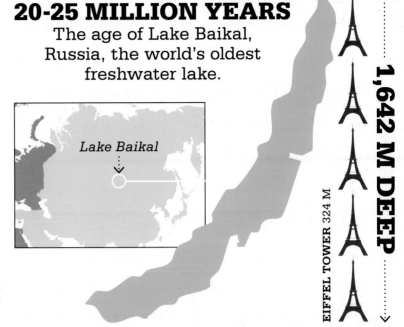

Lake Baikal

20%

23,000 CUBIC KM OF WATER

1,642 M DEEP

EIFFEL TOWER 324 M

FORMING THE HIMALAYAS
The world's highest mountain range, the Himalayas, was formed by the movement of the tectonic plates that make up the Earth's crust.

Around 70 million years ago, the Indian plate started pushing into the Eurasian plate.

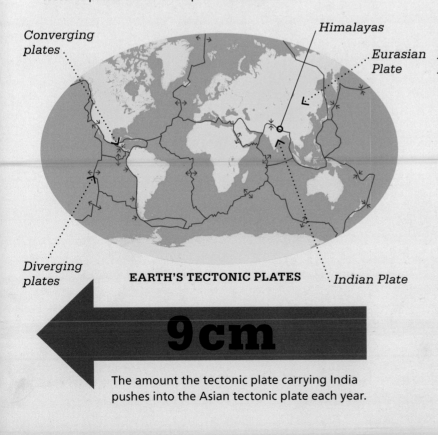

Converging plates

Himalayas

Eurasian Plate

Diverging plates

EARTH'S TECTONIC PLATES

Indian Plate

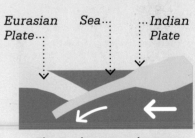

Eurasian Plate *Sea* *Indian Plate*

The sea between the two plates grew smaller and the sea floor was pushed up.

Himalayas

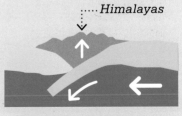

Eventually, the rocks of the sea floor were pushed up to form the Himalayas.

9cm

The amount the tectonic plate carrying India pushes into the Asian tectonic plate each year.

57

SUPER STATES

The countries of Asia include some of the largest in the world. They have enormous populations producing and consuming vast amounts of food and other products.

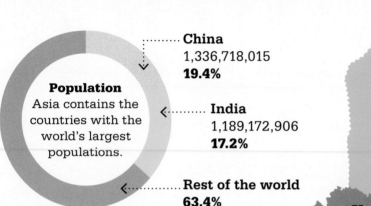

China
1,336,718,015
19.4%

India
1,189,172,906
17.2%

Rest of the world
63.4%

Population
Asia contains the countries with the world's largest populations.

RUSSIA

KAZAKHSTAN

Kazakhstan is the world's **largest** landlocked country

AZERBAIJAN
ARMENIA
UZBEKISTAN
KYRGYZSTAN
TURKMENISTAN
TAJIKISTAN
TURKEY
SYRIA
AFGHANISTAN
KASHMIR
LEBANON
IRAQ
IRAN
KUWAIT
QATAR
PAKISTAN
NEP
PALESTINE
BAHRAIN
ISRAEL
SAUDI
ARABIA
UAE
INDIA
OMAN
JORDAN
YEMEN
SRI LANKA

GREAT WALL

Between the 2nd century BCE and the 15th century CE, China built the world's longest wall to protect its northern border. Its main section stretches for

3,460 km

– more than three times the length of the UK.

3,460 KM

POPULATION GROWTH

Qatar is the fastest-growing country in the world.

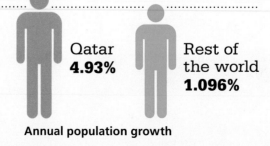

Qatar
4.93%

Rest of the world
1.096%

Annual population growth

Nepal's flag is not rectangular – it is formed from two red triangles.

ASIA'S WORKFORCE

China
795.4 million workers

India
498.4 million workers

USA
154.9 million workers

China and India are the world's biggest producers of rice.

Great Pyramid
6 MILLION TONNES

China
137 MILLION TONNES

India
96 MILLION TONNES

Between them they grow more than half of the world's rice – enough to create a pile 39 times the weight of the Great Pyramid.

RUSSIA

MONGOLIA

CHINA

Great Wall of China

NORTH KOREA

JAPAN

SOUTH KOREA

BHUTAN

BANGLADESH

LAOS

BURMA

THAILAND

VIETNAM

PHILIPPINES

CAMBODIA

BRUNEI

MALAYSIA

INDONESIA

EAST TIMOR

WORLD TOTAL

INDIA

India exports
2.16 million tonnes of beef,
nearly a quarter of the world's trade.

7,000 of Indonesia's **17,500 islands** are uninhabited.

59

AUSTRALIA AND OCEANIA

The region of Oceania is made up of the countries of Australia, New Zealand and more than a dozen nations found throughout the Pacific Ocean.

PAPUA NEW GUINEA
462,840 sq km
5.4%

NEW ZEALAND
270,692 sq km
3.2%

THE REST
89,268 sq km
1.1%

AUSTRALIA
7,702,501 sq km
90.3%

HIGHEST POINT
Mt Wilhelm, Papua New Guinea
4,509 m

The largest country in Oceania is Australia, which covers **7,702,501 sq km.**

OCEANIA

Australia has **28 times** the land area of **New Zealand,** but less than **twice** the coastline because it has far fewer indentations, bays and fjords.

CORAL REEF

Each coral reef is a community of tiny organisms called polyps, which can be 3–56 mm long. Some species of coral can have 3,000 polyps per square metre.

Mouth

Tentacle

20 mm
actual size

The Great Barrier Reef off the coast of eastern Australia is more than **2,000 km** long and covers an area of

348,000 sq km...

... about the same area as Germany.

Great Barrier Reef

LOWEST POINT

Lake Eyre, Australia
16 m below sea level

1.7%

The percentage of the world's land area made up by Oceania.

SUPER DIVERSITY

More species live in the Great Barrier Reef than in any other environment on Earth. The reef is not only home to 450 species of coral but also...

1,500 species of fish

4,000 species of snails and clams

6 of the world's seven species of sea turtle

TINY NATIONS

The Pacific is home to thousands of tiny countries and dependencies.

Wake Island
US territory
6.5 sq km
(321 football fields)

Nauru 21 sq km (1,037 football fields)

Tokelau
New Zealand territory
12 sq km
(593 football fields)

Coral Sea Islands
Australian territory
less than 3 sq km
(148 football fields)

Australian Rules Football field
20,250 sq m, 150 m x 135 m

PACIFIC PARADISE

The countries of Oceania are scattered over more than 10,000 islands that lie across the millions of square kilometres of the Pacific Ocean.

GUAM

PALAU

Yap

MICRONESIA

PAPUA NEW GUINEA

SOLOMO

700

The number of languages spoken in the country of Papua New Guinea. It has a population of just over **6 million.**

AUSTRALIA

REST OF THE CONTINENT

AUSTRALIA

39%

61%

LARGEST CITY
Sydney (Australia)
4,336,374

About 37 million people inhabit the islands and countries of Oceania, 22,651,000 of which live in Australia alone.

NEW ZEALAND

POPULATION GROWTH

The Cook Islands in the Pacific has the slowest growing population. In fact it is shrinking at a rate of -3.14%.

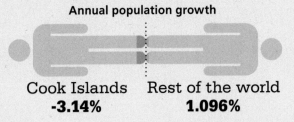

Annual population growth

Cook Islands
-3.14%

Rest of the world
1.096%

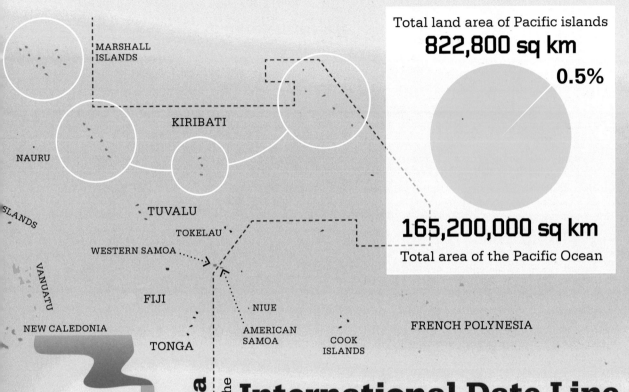

MARSHALL ISLANDS

KIRIBATI

NAURU

...SLANDS

TUVALU

TOKELAU

WESTERN SAMOA

VANUATU

FIJI

NIUE

NEW CALEDONIA

AMERICAN SAMOA

COOK ISLANDS

FRENCH POLYNESIA

TONGA

Total land area of Pacific islands
822,800 sq km

0.5%

165,200,000 sq km

Total area of the Pacific Ocean

13%
of New Zealand's electricity is produced by geothermal energy, most of it from the Taupo Volcanic Zone.

Oceania lies next to the

International Date Line,
which runs through the Pacific from the North Pole to the South Pole. The date changes by one day either side of the International Date Line. It is not a straight line, but passes around island groups, so they all have the same date.

Taupo Volcano

MOST SOUTHERLY CAPITAL CITY
Wellington, New Zealand
41°17'S

Hundreds of years ago, the tiny Pacific island of **Yap** used huge, doughnut shaped stones as money.

The largest are 3.5 m across, 0.5 m thick and can weigh 4 tonnes.

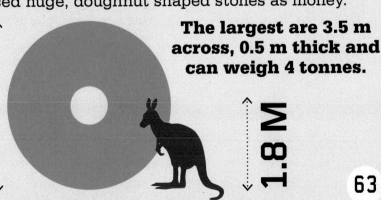

3.5 M

1.8 M

ANTARCTICA

Because of the Earth's tilt, the world's most southerly and coldest continent experiences six months of daylight followed by six months of darkness.

Antarctica contains no countries, but several areas are claimed and controlled by other nations, including the UK, Norway, Australia, New Zealand, France, Chile and Argentina.

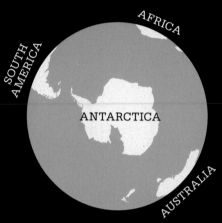

AFRICA

SOUTH AMERICA

ANTARCTICA

AUSTRALIA

HIGHEST POINT
Vinson Massif
4,697 m

2,450 m

Antarctica covers 14.2 million sq km – nearly twice the area of Australia. Only 280,000 sq km of this is not covered with ice.

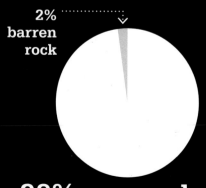

2% barren rock

829.84 m

98% covered in ice

Antarctica's ice sheet contains 29 million cubic km of ice – 90 per cent of the world's total glacial ice. **It has an average thickness of 2,450 m – three times the height of the Burj Khalifa (Dubai), the tallest building in the world to date.**

TEMPERATURE RANGES

Antarctica is the world's coldest place. Average temperatures range from just +1°C near the coast during summer, to a freezing -80°C and less in winter.

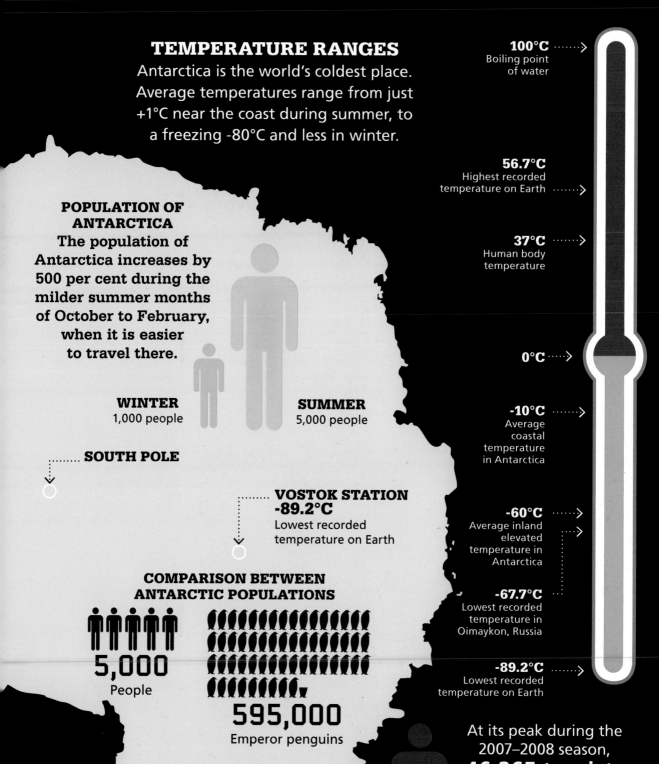

100°C ······> Boiling point of water

56.7°C Highest recorded temperature on Earth ······>

37°C ······> Human body temperature

0°C ······>

-10°C ······> Average coastal temperature in Antarctica

-60°C ······> Average inland elevated temperature in Antarctica ······>

-67.7°C Lowest recorded temperature in Oimaykon, Russia

-89.2°C ······> Lowest recorded temperature on Earth

POPULATION OF ANTARCTICA

The population of Antarctica increases by 500 per cent during the milder summer months of October to February, when it is easier to travel there.

WINTER 1,000 people

SUMMER 5,000 people

SOUTH POLE

VOSTOK STATION -89.2°C
Lowest recorded temperature on Earth

COMPARISON BETWEEN ANTARCTIC POPULATIONS

5,000 People

595,000 Emperor penguins

At its peak during the 2007–2008 season, **46,265 tourists** visited Antarctica, compared to 76 million who visited France, the world's most popular tourist destination.

POWERFUL MACHINES

Even the toughest job can be made easier by using a simple machine, such as a lever or a pulley. They can also be combined to create complex and incredibly powerful machines and vehicles.

LEVERS

A lever uses a long bar and a pivot, or fulcrum, to move a load. Moving the pivot closer to the load means you need less effort to lift it. Levers are found in diggers and cranes.

LOAD = 2

EFFORT = 1

pivot

1 metre   2 metres

GEARS

Gears are found in most vehicles, including bicycles. They transmit force to the wheels. The larger the gear on the rear wheel of a bike, the smaller the amount the wheel will turn. Large gears make it easier to pedal up a hill.

Large gear

Small gear

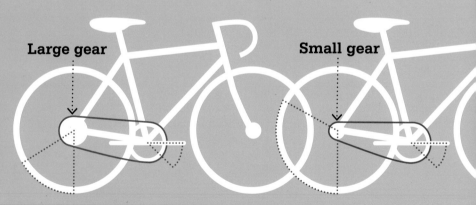

18 Large trucks have up to 18 gears to transmit power from their engines to the wheels so that the truck can pull a heavy load.

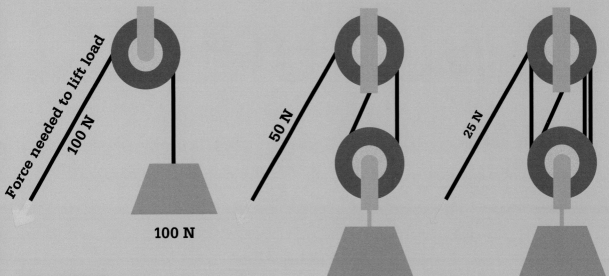

Force needed to lift load

100 N

100 N

50 N

100 N

25 N

100 N

PULLEYS

Pulleys are found on cranes and they use wheels and ropes to lift heavy objects. The more times a rope is fed through a pulley system, the easier it is to lift the load. Forces are measured in units called newtons (N).

Small force

Large force

long distance pushed

short distance moved

20,000 TONNES

THE SAFE LIFTING CAPACITY OF THE WORLD'S STRONGEST CRANE. CALLED TAISUN, IT IS LOCATED IN THE YANTAI RAFFLES SHIPYARD IN CHINA.

ATTRACT AND REPEL

Magnets will attract each other or repel each other depending on the orientation of their poles. This attracting and repelling can be used to pick up metal objects in a junkyard, or it can make a train hover above a magnetic track.

HYDRAULIC CYLINDERS

Hydraulics use liquids to transfer a force from one cylinder to another. A small force on a thin cylinder can create a large force on a thick cylinder. However, the force will only move the piston in the thick cylinder a short distance. Hydraulic cylinders are found on the arms of diggers or the hoppers of tipper trucks.

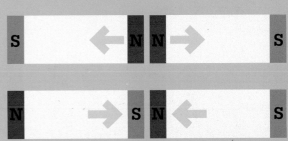

POWER UP!

Choosing the right energy source is vital to powering machines. The wind may be good enough to push a boat, but planes need a propeller or a powerful jet to fly, while space vehicles need a rocket.

PETROL CYCLE

The up-and-down action in a petrol engine cylinder is turned into a spinning movement by the crankshaft. Each time the crankshaft makes a complete circle is called a revolution. This type of engine is called an internal combustion engine, and they are found in cars, trucks and motorbikes.

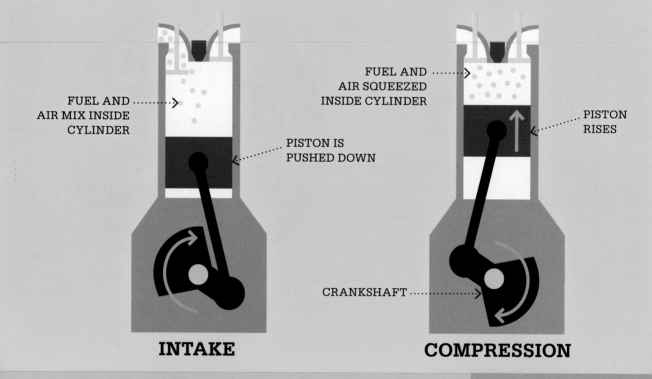

FUEL AND AIR MIX INSIDE CYLINDER

PISTON IS PUSHED DOWN

INTAKE

FUEL AND AIR SQUEEZED INSIDE CYLINDER

PISTON RISES

CRANKSHAFT

COMPRESSION

PROPELLER

When a propeller spins around, it creates an area of high pressure behind it. This pushes the propeller and the aircraft forwards. Propellers are used on aircraft and on powered boats and ships.

ENGINE

JET ENGINE

A jet burns fuel to create a powerful blast of hot gases. These hot gases push the vehicle forwards. Jet engines are used on record-breaking cars and aircraft.

WIND POWER

The wind is often harnessed to power machines. A yacht uses sails to catch the wind and push it forwards. To stop a yacht from being blown sideways it has a keel sticking down into the water.

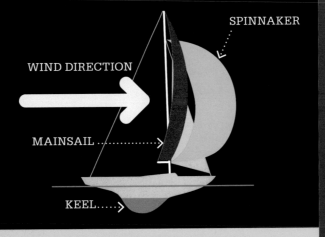

SPINNAKER

WIND DIRECTION

MAINSAIL

KEEL

18,000

The maximum number of revolutions per minute in a Formula One engine.

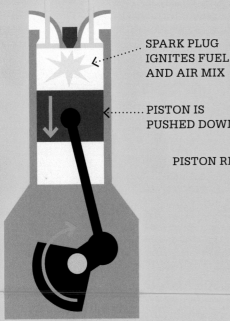

SPARK PLUG IGNITES FUEL AND AIR MIX

PISTON IS PUSHED DOWN

EXHAUST GASES ARE PUSHED OUT

PISTON RISES

POWER

EXHAUST

FUEL BURNT IN COMBUSTION CHAMBER

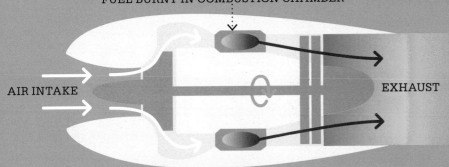

AIR INTAKE

EXHAUST

LIQUID OXYGEN

LIQUID FUEL

OXYGEN AND FUEL ARE SET ALIGHT

HOT GASES PUSH THE ROCKET FORWARDS

ROCKETS

Rockets work by burning a fuel with a substance called an oxidiser. In most space rockets, both the fuel and the oxidiser are stored as liquids before being mixed together and ignited. Rockets are also found on very fast aircraft and fireworks.

71

ON THE MOVE

How people travel about and what they choose to travel in has changed a lot over time and varies greatly from one country to another. A bicycle may be ideal for a short trip, but a high-speed train or a super-fast jet are better for international journeys.

PERCENTAGE OF THE UK POPULATION WITH ACCESS TO A CAR

1951 **14%**

2008 **78%**

USA

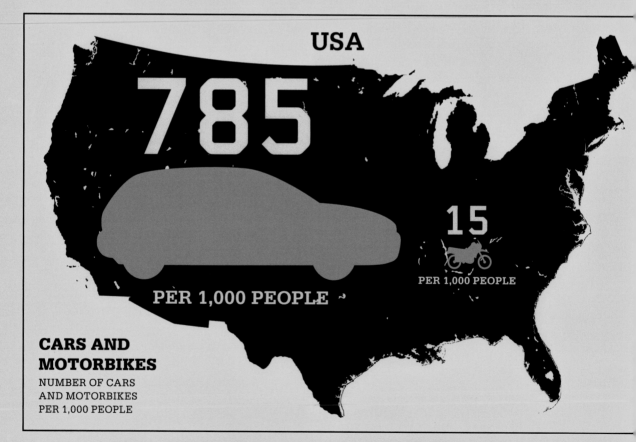

785

15

PER 1,000 PEOPLE

PER 1,000 PEOPLE

CARS AND MOTORBIKES

NUMBER OF CARS AND MOTORBIKES PER 1,000 PEOPLE

CROWDED ROADS

VEHICLES PER KM OF ROAD

USA — 33

ITALY — 10

LEBANON

HONG KONG

FUEL EFFICIENCY

AVERAGE FUEL COST PER PASSENGER BASED ON 800 KM JOURNEY

US$8.70 300 PASSENGERS

US$11.70 4 PASSENGERS

US$19.47 1 PASSENGER

US$39.66 175 PASSENGERS

500,000,000 BICYCLES IN CHINA

THAT'S 2.6 PEOPLE PER BIKE

INDIA

25

PER 1,000 PEOPLE

25

PER 1,000 PEOPLE

400,000,000 WORLDWIDE

V

1,400,000,000 WORLDWIDE

205

RECORD BREAKERS

Record-breaking machines are designed for one thing – to travel faster than anything else. They have special shapes that allow them to cut through the air or water as easily and as quickly as possible.

Record power

As well as a special shape, record breaking vehicles need a force to push them forwards. This force can come from a powerful jet engine, a roaring rocket or even the wind.

WATER SPEED RECORD
SPIRIT OF AUSTRALIA
511.11 KM/H

SAILING SPEED RECORD
HYDROPTÈRE
51.36 KNOTS

OLYMPIC SPRINTER
ABOUT 36 KM/H

THRUSTSSC (1997)
1,227.986 KM/H
ThrustSSC was fitted with two powerful jet fighter engines.

THRUST2 (1983)
1,019.47 KM/H

BLUE FLAME (1970)
1,001.667 KM/H

LAND SPEED RECORDS

88.8
The land speed record for a solar powered car stands at 88.8 km/h.

The shape of things

In order to move through the air or the water quickly, an object needs to be streamlined. A streamlined shape allows the air to flow around the vehicle easily. The more streamlined a vehicle is, the faster it can travel.

NON-STREAMLINED SHAPE

STREAMLINED SHAPE

AIR FLOW

TURBULENCE

Formula One racing is at the cutting edge of car design. Modern Formula One cars use a specially designed shape and 'wings' to travel as quickly as possible around a racetrack.

FORMULA ONE CAR **1950**

FORMULA ONE CAR **2012**

Comparison of speeds records

LAND SPEED RECORD
THRUSTSSC
1,227.986 KM/H

FLIGHT AIRSPEED RECORD
LOCKHEED BLACKBIRD
3,529.6 KM/H

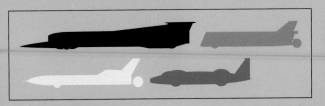

BLUEBIRD CN7 (1964)
644.96 KM/H

63.15

The first land speed record was set in 1898 at 63.15 km/h.

SLOWING DOWN

To slow down, vehicles need to use a force that works against their forward movement. To do this, they can either squeeze pads against their spinning wheels, deploy billowing parachutes behind them, or shoot out a powerful blast of gases.

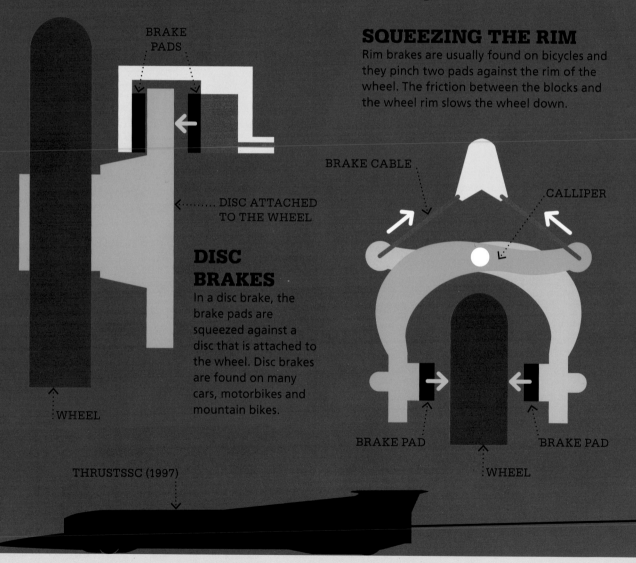

BRAKE PADS

SQUEEZING THE RIM

Rim brakes are usually found on bicycles and they pinch two pads against the rim of the wheel. The friction between the blocks and the wheel rim slows the wheel down.

.... DISC ATTACHED TO THE WHEEL

BRAKE CABLE

CALLIPER

DISC BRAKES

In a disc brake, the brake pads are squeezed against a disc that is attached to the wheel. Disc brakes are found on many cars, motorbikes and mountain bikes.

WHEEL

THRUSTSSC (1997)

BRAKE PAD

BRAKE PAD

WHEEL

12 METRES

The size of the parachute used to slow down a Space Shuttle after landing.

PARACHUTES

Parachutes work by increasing the air resistance, or drag, of an object as it moves. They are used to slow a person's fall from a plane or they are fitted to aircraft, drag racers and land speed record cars to slow them down.

DRUM BRAKES

Instead of pads, drum brakes push two curved 'shoes' against the inner surface of a drum that is attached to the wheel. This creates friction, which slows the drum and the wheel down. Drum brakes are fitted to cars and trucks.

BRAKE SHOE

BRAKE CABLE

DRUM

BRAKE SHOE

WHEEL

FORCE OF RETRO ROCKETS SLOWS DESCENT

GOING RETRO

Retro rockets fire a blast of gases in the same direction as the movement in order to slow a vehicle down. Some space vehicles use retro rockets to slow down their descent to a planet's surface.

The brakes on a **formula one** car can heat up to a temperature of **750°C** during a grand prix race.

THRUSTSSC BRAKING SYSTEM

ThrustSSC used a combination of disc brakes and two parachutes to slow it down. One small parachute was opened at 1,000 km/h to start the braking process. This was then released, and a second, larger parachute was opened once the car had slowed to 350 km/h.

PARACHUTE INCREASES AIR RESISTANCE TO SLOW DOWN THE VEHICLE

UP IN THE AIR

In order to soar into the sky, an aircraft can use specially shaped wings or it can make itself extra-light using heated air or special gases.

SPACESHIP ONE (2004) 112 KM

SpaceShipOne was carried high into the atmosphere by another aircraft, called White Knight. It was then released and fired its rockets to blast it to the edge of space.

LIFT

Aircraft wings have a special shape called an aerofoil. This creates higher pressure below the wing than above it, pushing the wing up. The wing is also angled so that it deflects air down and this also pushes the wing up.

AIR MOVES FASTER CREATING LOW PRESSURE

AIR MOVES SLOWER CREATING HIGH PRESSURE

LIFT

WING

WING FORCES AIR DOWN

LIGHTER THAN AIR

Hot-air balloons heat the air inside a large sac, called an envelope. This warmed air is less dense than the air outside so it rises, carrying the balloon with it. Airships use gases that are lighter than air to lift them up.

HOT AIR INSIDE SAC IS LESS DENSE THAN AIR OUTSIDE

50,000 M   40,000 M   30,000 M   20,000 M   10,000 M

AIRSHIP

AIR INSIDE BALLOON HEATED BY BURNERS

MIG-25 (1977)
HIGHEST JET
37,650 M

As well as holding the record for the highest flying jet aircraft, the MiG-25 was also one of the fastest military jets, capable of flying at three times the speed of sound.

CONCORDE
CRUISING ALTITUDE
18,000 M

This passenger aircraft flew at more than twice the speed of sound. It could fly from London to New York in three and a half hours, whereas a standard passenger jet takes seven to eight hours.

STRATO-LAB V (1961)
HIGHEST MANNED BALLOON
34,668 M

This balloon was filled with helium gas. It carried two people to a record-breaking altitude during a flight that lasted nine hours and 54 minutes.

HOT-AIR BALLOON (2004)
21,027 M

Vijaypat Singhania set the record for the highest hot-air balloon flight on 26 November 2005. His balloon was as tall as a 22-storey building.

MODERN PASSENGER JET
CRUISING ALTITUDE 10,000 M

Passenger airliners climb to a cruising altitude of around 10,000 m. At this height they are above any major turbulence caused by poor weather conditions closer to the ground.

79

FLYING GIANTS

Carrying heavy loads through the air needs some powerful flying machines. These giants use huge propellers, powerful jets or enormous bags of gas to get off the ground.

HEAVY LIFTING
MIL V-12
The world's largest helicopter was designed to lift 30,000 kg – that's about six elephants.

PASSENGER AIRSHIP
LZ 129 *HINDENBURG*
The *Hindenburg* was as tall as a 13-storey building, with a volume of 200,000 cubic metres – enough to fill 80 Olympic swimming pools.

CARGO AIRCRAFT
ANTONOV AN-225
The Antonov AN-225 is the world's heaviest aircraft. It has six powerful jet engines and a landing gear system with 32 wheels. It was designed to transport space rockets.

245 M
The overall length of the *Hindenburg*, longer than eight basketball courts.

1,600 M

The distance of the one and only flight performed by the Spruce Goose on 2 November 1947.

FLYING BOAT HUGHES H-4 SPRUCE GOOSE

The Hughes H-4 Spruce Goose had a wingspan of 97.5 m, which is more than twice the length of the Wright Brothers' first powered flight (36.5 m).

PASSENGER JET AIRBUS A380

The Airbus A380 is 72.7 m long – as long as two blue whales. It has two passenger decks and can carry more than 500 people.

ON TRACK

Record-breaking trains need powerful locomotives to pull them along. Over the years, these super-fast locomotives have been powered by steam, electricity and even by magnets.

HIGH-SPEED TRAIN LINES

High-speed trains need special tracks that reduce the amount of vibration and do not have level crossings. These tracks allow the trains to travel at more than 200 km/h. Some countries, such as Japan, have a large high-speed line network.

FRANCE 1,872 KM

GERMANY 1,285 KM

UK 113 KM

JAPAN 2,452 KM

USA 362 KM

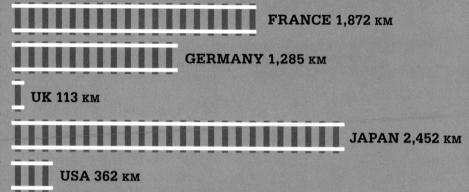

TGV
574.8 KM/H
Short for *Train à Grande Vitesse* (meaning 'high-speed train'), a test model of this electric-powered French locomotive set the record for the fastest wheeled train, reaching 574.8 km/h on 3 April 2007.

JR-MAGLEV
581 KM/H
The Japanese JR-Maglev set a record speed for a tracked vehicle of 581 km/h on 2 December 2003.

LONGEST TRAIN BHP FREIGHT TRAIN
21 JUNE 2001, WESTERN AUSTRALIA

683 WAGONS, **8** LOCOMOTIVES **7.353** KM LONG **99,700 TONNES**

The world's **earliest** railway dates from the **sixth century BC**. The Diolkos wagonway in Greece was just **6 km** long.

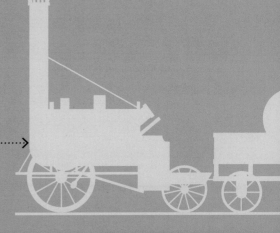

STEPHENSON'S *ROCKET* ⌁⌁⌁⌁⌁>

48 KM/H

The *Rocket* was built in 1829 to take part in the Rainhill Trials. These were tests to see which type of locomotive would work on one of the first train lines – the *Rocket* won.

MALLARD ⌁⌁⌁⌁⌁⌁>

202.6 KM/H

Built in 1938, the *Mallard* still holds the record for the world's fastest steam-powered locomotive.

1,139,615 KM

The total amount of railtrack in the entire world. The USA has 224,792 km of railtrack, Russia has 87,157 km and China has about 86,00 km.

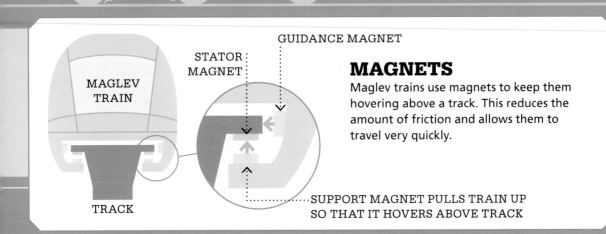

MAGLEV TRAIN

TRACK

STATOR MAGNET

GUIDANCE MAGNET

MAGNETS

Maglev trains use magnets to keep them hovering above a track. This reduces the amount of friction and allows them to travel very quickly.

SUPPORT MAGNET PULLS TRAIN UP SO THAT IT HOVERS ABOVE TRACK

WATER WORLD

Gigantic ocean-going ships are used to carry military aircraft, huge amounts of crude oil or thousands of passengers on a holiday cruise. They are some of the largest machines on the planet.

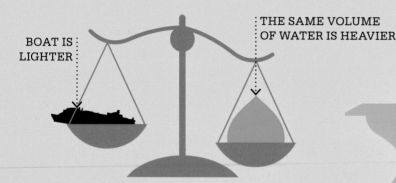

BOAT IS LIGHTER

THE SAME VOLUME OF WATER IS HEAVIER

WHY THINGS FLOAT
A ship floats because it weighs less than the same volume of water.

LONGEST SHIP *KNOCK NEVIS*
Measuring 458.25 m long, the *Knock Nevis* was the longest ship ever built. This enormous ship carried oil and was too big to sail through the English Channel, the Suez Canal and the Panama Canal.

PASSENGER SHIP *OASIS OF THE SEAS*
This enormous liner contains a casino, mini golf course, nightclubs and volleyball and basketball courts.

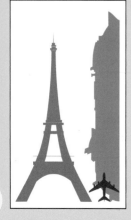

Oasis of the Seas has enough electrical cable to stretch between London and New York.

FIVE TIMES BIGGER THAN THE *TITANIC*

BIGGEST PROPELLER

The world's largest propeller has a mass of

130 TONNES.

This six-bladed monster is used to power the *Emma Maersk*, the biggest container ship on the planet. The propeller can push this massive ship and its load of nearly 15,000 containers at a cruising speed of 27 knots (50 km/h).

9.6 M

NAVAL VESSEL
USS *ENTERPRISE*

This aircraft carrier is the longest naval vessel in the world. It is 342 m long and has a crew of nearly 6,000, including 1,800 pilots and aircrew.

TONNAGE 225,282
LENGTH 360 M
HEIGHT 72 M ABOVE WATER LINE
DECKS 16 PASSENGER DECKS
SPEED 22.6 KNOTS (41.9 KM/H)
CAPACITY 6,296 MAXIMUM **CREW** 2,165

FIVE

The number of swimming pools on board the *Oasis of the Seas*.

LONGER THAN THREE FOOTBALL PITCHES

FREE DIVING 214 M
SCUBA DIVING 330 M
ATMOSPHERIC DIVING SUIT 610 M
MILITARY SUBMARINE 1,300 M
COLOSSAL SQUID 2,200 M
SPERM WHALE 3,000 M
WRECK OF *TITANIC* 3,780 M

The wreck of the *Titanic* was found in September 1985. It lies in two pieces with debris scattered over 5 square kilometres.

BENEATH THE WAVES

Deep beneath the surface of the ocean, water pressures are so great that they could squash a person flat. Vehicles that can dive to these depths are specially designed to withstand these forces.

DIVING AND SURFACING

Submarines dive and rise in the water by altering their buoyancy. This is their ability to float. They alter their buoyancy by pumping air and water into and out of special tanks.

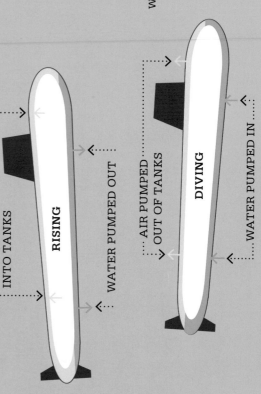

AIR PUMPED INTO TANKS
RISING
WATER PUMPED OUT

AIR PUMPED OUT OF TANKS
DIVING
WATER PUMPED IN

1620

The first-ever submarine was built by Cornelius van Drebbel around 1620 and travelled below the surface of the Thames to depths of 5 metres.

Record depth achieved by the *Trieste* on its descent into the Mariana Trench in January 1960.

10,916 M

DEEPEST RECORDED DIVE BY *TRIESTE*

1775 *TURTLE*

The *Turtle* was the first submersible ever used in combat. It was built by American forces to attack explosives to British ships during the War of Independence (1775–83) and could move at about 2.7 knots (5 km/h).

1800 *NAUTILUS*

This early French submarine was designed to attack warships. It was built from copper sheets over an iron frame and had a speed of about 2 knots (3.7 km/h).

1936 TYPE VII U-BOAT

Short for *Unterseeboot* (German for 'undersea boat'), U-boats were used during World War I (1914–18) and World War II (1939–45) to attack convoys carrying supplies. The Type VII U-boat could sail at 7.6 knots (14 km/h) when submerged.

2000 VIRGINIA CLASS

This attack submarine is powered by a nuclear reactor and has a crew of 135 people. It is 115 m long and has an underwater speed of 25 knots (46 km/h).

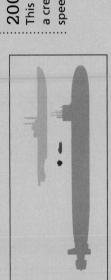

MONSTER MACHINES

Industrial vehicles are designed to move massive loads from one place to another. This could be earth and rubble, petrol or even space rockets. Whatever they carry, these vehicles are designed to be big enough and powerful enough to handle huge weights.

BIGGEST TIPPER TRUCK
LIEBHERR T 282B

This massive truck is designed to carry a load of more than 350 tonnes – that is nearly 70 elephants! It uses hydraulics (see page 69) to push its hopper up to empty a load.

WORLD'S LARGEST MOVEABLE INDUSTRIAL MACHINE

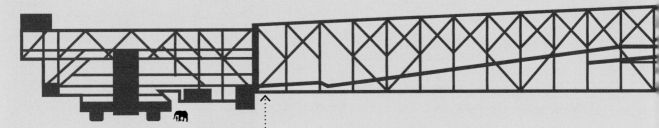

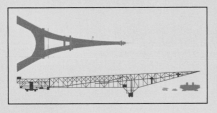

OVERBURDEN CONVEYOR BRIDGE F60

Built to work in a coal mine in Germany, this enormous machine is 502 m long and has a mass of 13,600 tonnes – more than 75 blue whales! It is designed to carry rocks and earth away from the coal seam.

BIGGEST BULLDOZER
D575A-3SD

This monster machine is fitted with a huge blade on the front that can push 96 cubic metres of earth and rubble at a time.

14.91 M

The height of the Leibherr T 282B when the hopper is raised to its maximum.

MOBILE LAUNCH PLATFORM

Built to transport the massive Saturn V rockets (see pages 92–93), this giant measures 49 m by 41 m. When it carried an unfuelled Space Shuttle, it had a mass of 5,000 tonnes.

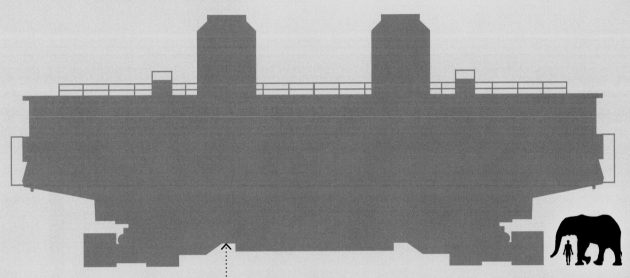

ROAD TRAIN
MACK TITAN

The world's longest road train to be pulled by a single unit measured 1,474.3 m long. It consisted of 112 trailers and had a mass of 1,300 tonnes and was driven just 100 m on 18 February 2006.

50,000 TONNES

The amount of material the Overburden Conveyor Bridge F60 can move in an hour. That is enough to cover a football pitch to a depth of up to 8 m.

DIGGING DEEP

These digging machines use claw-like shovels, enormous spinning wheels or rotating discs covered in sharp teeth to cut, slice and tear through rock and earth.

LARGEST HYDRAULIC SHOVEL
TEREX RH400
Moved by a powerful hydraulics system (see page 69), the enormous shovel on this excavator can lift 86 tonnes of rubble – that is 17 elephants.

LARGEST LAND VEHICLE
BAGGER 288
Used in a coal mine in Germany, this machine can fill 2,400 coal wagons in a single day. It is 220 m long.

The enormous digging wheel measures 21.6 m across and has 18 huge buckets.

<· · · · · · · · · · · BUCKET

LARGEST DRAGLINE EXCAVATOR
BIG MUSKIE
This excavator used pulleys and levers (see pages 68–69) to move its enormous bucket, which was big enough to fit two single-decker buses. It operated at a mine in the USA from 1969 until 1991.

30 M
The depth of earth the Bagger 288 could cover a football pitch with in a single day.

TUNNEL BORING MACHINE
The largest tunnel boring machine designed to cut through hard rock measured 14.4 m across. It was used to dig a tunnel beneath Niagara Falls, Canada, as part of a hydroelectric power station.

96 M
The height of the Bagger 288 – as tall as a 25-storey building.

BLAST OFF!

Rockets are used to power vehicles to incredible speeds. They are the only energy source that can push a vehicle high into the atmosphere and even out into space.

IN STAGES

Many space rockets come in parts, known as stages. Each stage has its own rocket engines and fuel supply. When a stage has run out of fuel, it is ejected, making the whole rocket lighter. The engines on the next stage ignite and the rocket climbs higher.

SPACE PLANE

SpaceShipTwo is designed to be carried high into the atmosphere by another aircraft before it is released. It then ignites its rockets to blast to the edge of space, before gliding back down to land.

ZERO GRAVITY AT MAXIMUM HEIGHT

RE-ENTRY WITH FOLDED WINGS

UNPOWERED GLIDE

90-SECOND CLIMB AT 4,000 KM/H

SPACESHIPTWO AND CARRIER AIRCRAFT SEPARATE

3. UPPER STAGE IGNITES ROCKET AND RELEASES LOWER STAGE.

2. ROCKET BOOSTERS RELEASED HIGH IN THE ATMOSPHERE.

1. ROCKET BLASTS OFF WITH BOOSTERS STRAPPED TO ITS SIDES.

SATURN V USA

The mighty Saturn V holds the records for being the tallest and heaviest rocket ever built and for delivering the heaviest payload. Thirteen of these giants were launched, carrying people to the Moon and space stations into orbit.

SPACE SHUTTLE USA

Used to launch satellites and space probes from 1981 to 2011, Space Shuttles were reusable. They were strapped to enormous fuel tanks and powerful boosters, which were released high in the atmosphere.

ARIANNE 5 EUROPE

This rocket has two powerful boosters strapped to its sides, as well as a main engine. It releases these boosters when they have used up all of their fuel.

VOSTOCK USSR

The Vostok rockets were developed from long-range missiles. The first artificial satellite, Sputnik, was launched into orbit by one of these rockets.

MERCURY USA

The Mercury space program was the first successful American attempt to send people into space. Mercury capsules were launched on top of Atlas rockets.

V2 GERMANY

This long-range missile was developed by Germany during World War II. It was designed to blast high into the atmosphere and had a range of 320 km.

THE LARGEST ROCKET EVER BUILT IS THE SATURN V – IT WAS 110.6 M TALL.

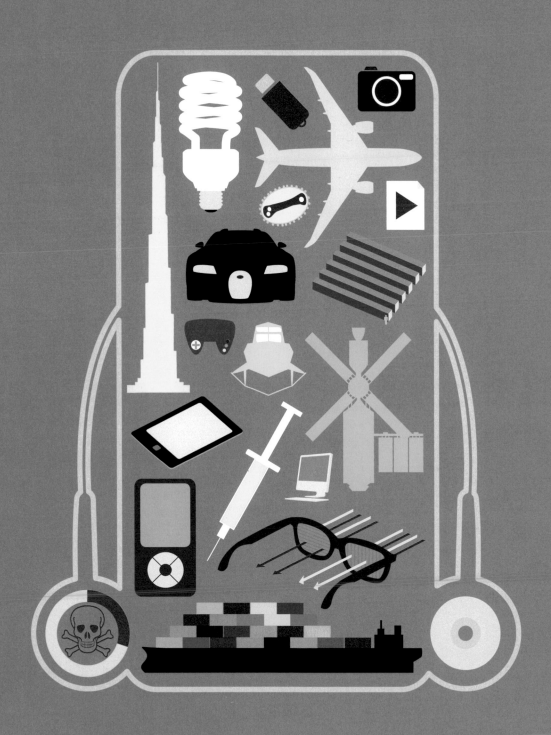

COMPUTING POWER

Computer information is measured in bytes. While the earliest personal computers (PCs) could handle a few thousand bytes, today's computers can process many times this amount in the blink of an eye.

Memory size

Global data traffic

An estimated **3.5 zettabytes (3,584 exabytes)** per year – enough to fill 750 billion DVDs, creating a pile long enough to stretch to the Moon and back!

1 MEGABYTE (1 million bytes)   **1 GIGABYTE**

1 GIGABYTE (1,024 MB)   **1 TERABYTE** (1,024 GB)

GB = ✓ ▶   **2 GB =** 🏃

MOBILE GROWTH

In 2013, the number of mobile devices (smartphones and tablets) exceeded the number of desktop and laptop computers for the first time.

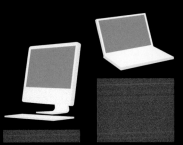

iPads make up **30%** of this market

2%   **10%**   **30%**

Growth in sales per year

TITAN SUPERCOMPUTER

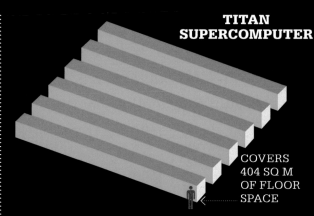

COVERS 404 SQ M OF FLOOR SPACE

Located in Tennessee, USA, it was built in 2012 by the US Energy Department for scientific research and can perform

20,000 TRILLION
calculations per second.

1 TERABYTE

1 PETABYTE

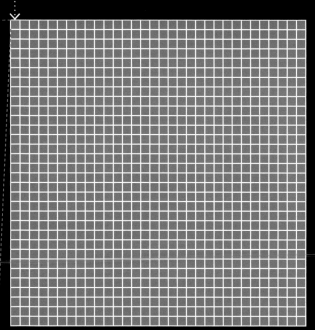

1 PETABYTE (1,024 TB)   **1 EXABYTE** (1,024 PB)

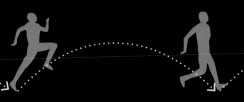

... longer than the triple jump world record (18.29 m)

4.7GB = one standard DVD

THE INTERNET

Since its creation in 1969, the internet has grown into an amazing source of information and entertainment. The amount of data is constantly growing, so the facts on these pages are just a snapshot of the internet's development.

WHO IS ONLINE?

Percentage of internet users by area in 2012

- NORTH AMERICA **78.6%**
- LATIN AMERICA AND CARIBBEAN **42.9%**
- EUROPE **63.2%**
- ASIA AND MIDDLE EAST **28.1%**
- AFRICA **15.6%**
- OCEANIA AND AUSTRALIA **67.6%**

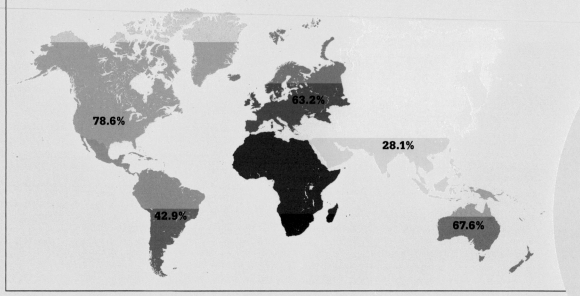

78.6% 63.2% 28.1% 42.9% 67.6%

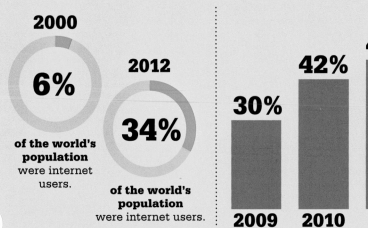

2000

6%

of the world's **population** were internet users.

2012

34%

of the world's **population** were internet users.

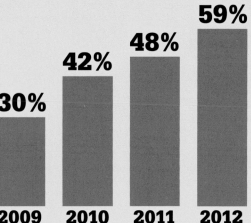

30% 2009
42% 2010
48% 2011
59% 2012

The rise of video
Bars show the percentage of internet traffic taken up by streamed videos.

INTERNET CONNECTIVITY

The growth in the number of devices connected to the internet.

● IN 2003, THERE WERE ABOUT **500 MILLION** DEVICES CONNECTED TO THE INTERNET.

BY 2010, THERE WERE **12.5 BILLION** (1.8 FOR EVERY PERSON ON THE PLANET).

BY 2015, IT IS PREDICTED THERE WILL BE **25 BILLION** (3.5 FOR EVERY PERSON ON THE PLANET).

BY 2020, IT IS PREDICTED THERE WILL BE **50 BILLION** (6.7 FOR EVERY PERSON ON THE PLANET).

THE RISE OF MOBILE

HOW THE WAY WE ACCESS THE INTERNET IS CHANGING
Mobile broadband subscriptions (billions)

Year	Subscriptions
2008	0.1
2012	1.4
2015	3.6
2017	5.0

INCREASE IN MOBILE TRAFFIC
Information transferred globally per month (in exabytes)

Mobile PCs and tablets
2011 **0.2**
BY 2017 **4.4**

Mobile phones
2011 **0.17**
BY 2017 **3.6**

HOW PEOPLE ACCESS THE INTERNET AROUND THE WORLD:

Mobile devices now account for **12%** of global internet traffic.

This is up from **1%** in 2009.

But in **India**, they account for **52%**.

99

THE TELEPHONE

The invention of the telephone may have allowed people in different places to have a conversation, but modern phones have even more ways for people to communicate, including email and text messages.

THE FIRST TELEPHONE CALL

The very first telephone call was made on 10 March 1876. Alexander Graham Bell called his assistant in another room using the message

"Mr Watson! Come here! I want you."

The world's biggest working telephone was **2.47 m high**, **6.06 m long** and weighed **3.5 tonnes**. It was built in 1988 by a Dutch insurance company to celebrate its 80th anniversary.

MOBILE PLANET

How the number of mobile phones has increased since 2001.

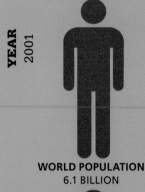

YEAR 2001

WORLD POPULATION
6.1 BILLION

MOBILE PHONES
950 MILLION

YEAR 2005

WORLD POPULATION
6.5 BILLION

MOBILE PHONES
2.2 BILLION

YEAR 2013

WORLD POPULATION
7.15 BILLION (EST)

MOBILE PHONES
6.9 BILLION (EST)

MOBILE PHONE EVOLUTION

The first mobile phones were the size of bricks and could only make calls. Modern smart phones are lightweight and come equipped with cameras, music players and more.

Nokia 3310 **2000**
- **height:** 113 mm • **weight:** 133 g
- **talk time:** 4 hr 30 min • **standby:** 260 hrs
- **memory:** 250 numbers • **extras:** SMS, ringtones, calculator, games

Apple iPhone **2007**
- **height:** 115 mm • **weight:** 135 g
- **talk time:** 8 hrs • **standby:** 250 hrs
- **memory:** 16 gb • **extras:** SMS, ringtones, calculator, stopwatch, games, camera, music player, touchscreen, internet browser, email, apps

Motorola Dynatac 8000X **1983**
- **height:** 300 mm • **weight:** 785 g • **talk time:** 1 hr • **standby:** 8 hrs
- **memory:** 30 numbers • **extras:** none

Nokia 2110 **1993**
- **height:** 148 mm • **weight:** 236 g
- **talk time:** 2 hr 40 min • **standby:** 30 h
- **memory:** 125 numbers • **extras:** SMS

Samsung Galaxy SIII **2012**
- **height:** 137 mm • **weight:** 133 g • **talk time:** 11 hours • **extras:** SMS,
- **standby:** 790 hours • **memory:** 32 gb ringtones, calculator, games, camera, music player, touchscreen, internet browser, email, apps, voice activation

The first phone call using a cellular network was made in the USA on 3 April 1973 by Martin Cooper of Motorola.

TEXTING FACTS
First text sent in 1992 – "Merry Christmas"

In 2010, China sent
825,000,000,000
SMS text messages

GADGETS

The latest gadgets can hold vast entertainment libraries. A 16 GB tablet computer has enough memory for 10 movies, 4,000 songs or 32,000 photographs.

NUMBER OF IPODS SOLD

2002
600,000

2003
2 MILLION

2004
10 MILLION

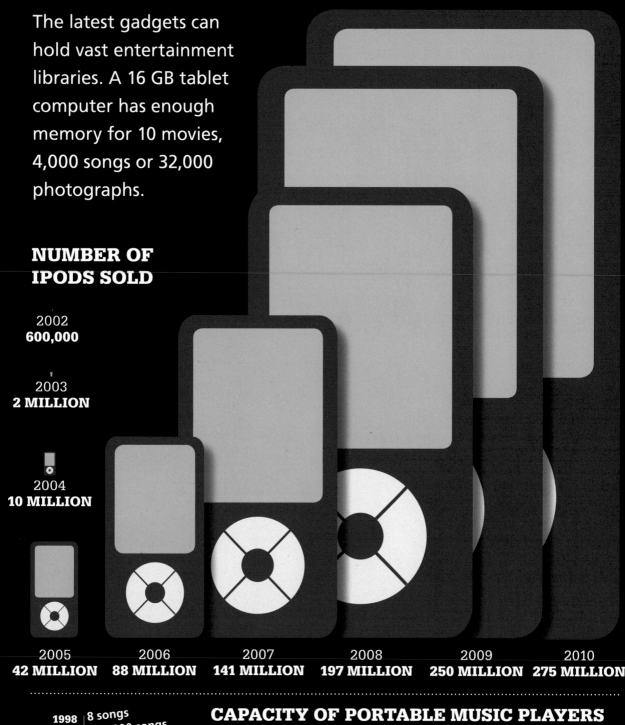

2005	2006	2007	2008	2009	2010
42 MILLION	**88 MILLION**	**141 MILLION**	**197 MILLION**	**250 MILLION**	**275 MILLION**

CAPACITY OF PORTABLE MUSIC PLAYERS

1998 8 songs
2001 1,000 songs
2003 7,500 songs
2004 10,000 songs
2005 20,000 songs
2012

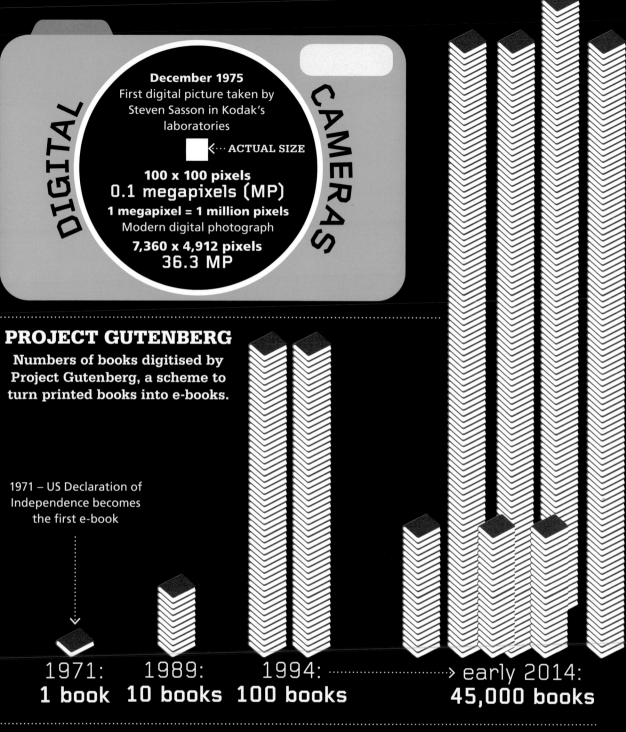

DIGITAL CAMERAS

December 1975
First digital picture taken by Steven Sasson in Kodak's laboratories

◼ <···· ACTUAL SIZE

100 x 100 pixels
0.1 megapixels (MP)
1 megapixel = 1 million pixels
Modern digital photograph
7,360 x 4,912 pixels
36.3 MP

PROJECT GUTENBERG

Numbers of books digitised by Project Gutenberg, a scheme to turn printed books into e-books.

1971 – US Declaration of Independence becomes the first e-book

1971:
1 book

1989:
10 books

1994:
100 books

early 2014:
45,000 books

100

114

In May 2012, Kindle e-book sales overtook Amazon print sales for the first time, with

114 E-BOOKS
sold for every
100 HARDBACK AND PAPERBACK BOOKS.

40,000 songs

ENTERTAINMENT

Technological advances have made the world's favourite forms of entertainment even more popular. The 3-D film *Avatar* became the most successful film ever in 2009, earning US$1 billion in just 17 days.

TV
DIGITAL vs ANALOGUE

Analogue signals are like a wave and vary in size and shape. Digital signals are either on or off. The pattern of the ons and offs is decided by the information. Digital signals carry more information, creating a sharper, high-definition TV picture.

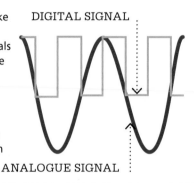

DIGITAL SIGNAL

ANALOGUE SIGNAL

STANDARD
720 X 576
pixels

High-definition televisions (HDTVs) have more pixels than standard TVs, producing clearer, sharper images.

HIGH-DEFINITION
1920 X 1080
pixels

72%
OF HOUSEHOLDS IN THE USA PLAY **COMPUTER OR VIDEO GAMES**.

VIDEO GAMES

As of January 2014, players on the online game *WORLD OF WARCRAFT* had notched a combined playing time of over **6 MILLION YEARS!**

49%
OF HOUSEHOLDS IN THE USA **OWN A GAMES CONSOLE** (AND THOSE THAT DO OWN TWO ON AVERAGE).

HOW 3-D MOVIES WORK

3-D movies combine two images that are slightly different from each other. Special glasses only let light from one image reach each eye. Your brain then puts these two images together to produce a three-dimensional effect.

DOUBLE IMAGE ON SCREEN

THE LENS IN EACH EYEHOLE ONLY LETS LIGHT FROM ONE IMAGE THROUGH

LIGHT FROM BOTH IMAGES

LEFT EYE RECEIVES ONE IMAGE

RIGHT EYE RECEIVES ONE IMAGE

SATELLITE BROADCAST

It is possible to watch live TV images around the world using satellites. Powerful antennae beam images up to satellites orbiting hundreds of kilometres above the Earth. These then beam the images to other parts of the world.

SATELLITE

ANTENNAE

HOME

The first 3-D film shown to a paying audience was *THE POWER OF LOVE* in **1922**.

The first colour 3-D film was *HOUSE OF WAX* in **1953**, a horror movie starring Vincent Price.

44,000
The approximate number of radio stations around the world. There are even
THREE
broadcasting in
ANTARCTICA.

IN THE HOME

Time-saving appliances have been making our lives easier since the 19th century. In recent times, technology has helped to create more environmentally friendly gadgets.

SOLAR PANELS CAN BE USED TO PROVIDE 75% OF A TYPICAL HOUSEHOLD'S ANNUAL ELECTRICITY

SMALL TURBINES CAN PRODUCE NEARLY 14,000 KW/H OF ELECTRICITY A YEAR

WATER STORAGE TANK

DUAL FLUSH TOILETS CAN SAVE 26,000 L OF WATER A YEAR

TRIPLE GLAZING CAN REDUCE THE AMOUNT OF HEAT LOST THROUGH A WINDOW BY 75%

RAINWATER CAN BE COLLECTED TO WATER GARDENS

ENERGY EFFICIENT BULBS LAST 10 TIMES LONGER THAN INCANDESCENT ONES

EFFICIENT HOMES

There are many ways of making a building more energy efficient. These range from collecting rainwater and reducing water use to fitting solar panels to produce electricity.

NEW ENERGY EFFICIENT FRIDGES USE 75% LESS ENERGY THAN OLDER MODELS. OVER A YEAR, THAT AMOUNTS TO ENOUGH ENERGY TO WATCH TV FOR 300 DAYS.

GREY WATER FROM SINKS AND WASHING MACHINES CAN BE USED TO WATER PLANTS AND FLUSH TOILETS

MICROWAVES

A microwave oven causes water molecules inside food to vibrate. This heats the food.

MICROWAVES

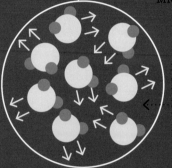

MICROWAVES CAUSE WATER MOLECULES TO VIBRATE PRODUCING HEAT

PRESERVING

Refrigerators cool food, keeping it fresh for longer. However, foodstuffs go off at different rates, so it is important to know how long each one can be kept in the fridge for.

REFRIGERATION TIME SCALES

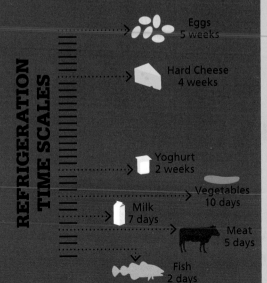

Eggs
5 weeks

Hard Cheese
4 weeks

Yoghurt
2 weeks

Vegetables
10 days

Milk
7 days

Meat
5 days

Fish
2 days

LIGHTING

Just **5%** of the energy used by an incandescent light bulb is used to make light. The rest produces heat.

Energy efficient light bulbs use **90%** less energy.

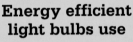

If each US household replaced one incandescent bulb with an energy efficient one, it would save enough energy to light

300,000,000

homes for an entire year and eliminate

4,000,000,000 KG

of greenhouse gases – equivalent to the emissions of 80,000 cars.

THE CAR

More than 60 million cars are made every year. Advances in technology have seen cars zoom from walking pace to blistering speeds, and cross continents powered only by the Sun.

FIRST CAR

The first petrol-powered car was built by German Karl Benz in 1885–6. The Benz Patent-Motorwagen had three wheels and was powered by an internal combustion engine.

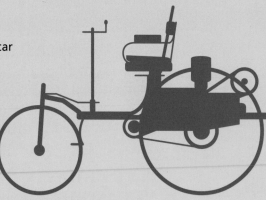

BENZ PATENT-MOTORWAGEN

1 CYLINDER, 954 CC
0.6 HP AT 250 RPM
TOP SPEED:
ABOUT 13 KM/H

BUGATTI VEYRON
(16.4 SUPER SPORT)

The fastest production car in the world is the Bugatti Veyron. A production car is one that is on sale to the public and has not been altered for racing.

16 CYLINDERS, 7,993 CC
1,183 BHP AT 6,400 RPM
0–100 KM/H IN 2.5 SECS
0–200 KM/H IN 6.7 SECS
0–300 KM/H IN 14.6 SECS
TOP SPEED 431 KM/H

A Veyron set the official speed record for a production car of **431.071 km/h on 3 July 2010**.

A tennis court is **23.78 metres** long.

The Bugatti would stop from 100 km/h in **31.4 metres**.
A normal family car would need **73 metres**.

START
DARWIN

World Solar Challenge held in Australia

FINISH
ADELAIDE

Using just solar power, cars entering the biennial **World Solar Challenge** complete a distance of

3,000 KM

in less than **five days**. These cars use less power than a hair dryer, but can travel at 88 km/h.

A **1966 Volvo** set the record for having the highest mileage of any car. By December 2010, it had covered more than

4,586,630 KM

That is equivalent to driving nearly **115** times around the globe.

It is still driven today and covers 160,000 km a year to car shows around the world.

VW BEETLE (22,650,000 SOLD TO DATE)

VW GOLF (27,190,000 SOLD TO DATE)

FORD F-SERIES (33,900,000 SOLD TO DATE)

TOYOTA COROLLA (ABOUT 35,000,000 SOLD TO DATE)

WORLD'S BEST-SELLING CARS

TRAINS AND BOATS

The need to carry heavier loads has seen the development of boats almost 500 m long and trains more than six times that length.

ROLLER

WHEELS

TILTING TRAINS

Some trains travel up to 15 per cent faster by tilting their carriages as they go round corners. This allows them to maintain a higher speed.

LONGEST FREIGHT TRAIN

Stretching for 7.353 km, the longest ever train was formed of eight diesel-electric locomotives, which pulled 682 cars. It was operated in 2001 by the BHP mining company and used to haul iron ore 275 km from mines to the coast in Western Australia.

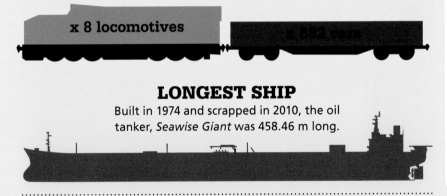

x 8 locomotives

x 682 cars

TILT BEAM

LONGEST SHIP

Built in 1974 and scrapped in 2010, the oil tanker, *Seawise Giant* was 458.46 m long.

CONTAINER SHIPS

The latest giant container ships can carry enough containers to hold 36,000 cars, or 863 million tins of beans.

1950s 500–800 containers

2013 18,000 containers

The biggest locomotive ever was the steam powered **Union Pacific's Big Boy**, which operated from 1941–1959. It could pull a train weighing 3,500 tonnes.

HOVERCRAFT

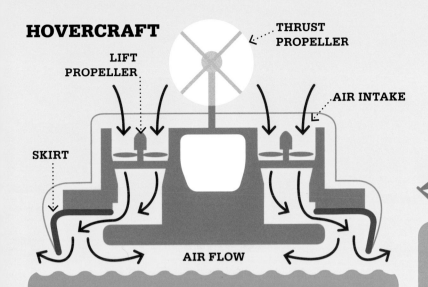

LIFT PROPELLER

THRUST PROPELLER

AIR INTAKE

SKIRT

AIR FLOW

HYDROFOIL

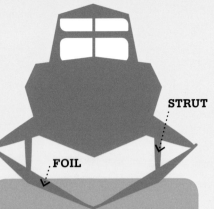

STRUT

FOIL

HOVERCRAFT

A hovercraft floats on a layer of air that is pushed downwards by the lift propellers. A 'curtain' of waterproof material called the skirt helps to keep this air underneath the hovercraft. The thrust propeller then pushes the hovercraft forwards.

HYDROFOIL

As the boat moves, water flowing over the foil produces lift, which pushes the boat out of the water. This greatly reduces the amount of friction, allowing the boat's engines to push it along very quickly.

HEAVY LIFT SHIP

These ships are designed to lift up other vessels that have been damaged and cannot sail on their own. The heavy lift ship then carries the damaged vessel back to port where it can be fixed.

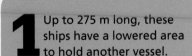
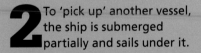
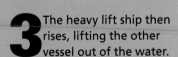

1 Up to 275 m long, these ships have a lowered area to hold another vessel.

2 To 'pick up' another vessel, the ship is submerged partially and sails under it.

3 The heavy lift ship then rises, lifting the other vessel out of the water.

That is the weight of nearly **20 adult blue whales.**

FLIGHT

Since the first powered flight in 1903, which travelled just 37 m, planes have been developed that can travel non-stop all the way around the world – a distance of more than 42,000 km.

THE ICARUS CUP

The Icarus Cup is a competition for human-powered aircraft. In 2012, the winning plane, *Airglow*, completed the 1-km-long course in just over 2 minutes.

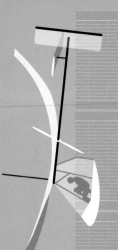

1 KM IS LONGER THAN NINE AMERICAN FOOTBALL PITCHES

SOLAR IMPULSE

The *Solar Impulse* is a solar powered plane that can fly at night by storing the Sun's energy. It holds the record for manned solar powered flight, flying for more than 26 hours, 10,000 m above Switzerland.

IT HAS **12,000 SOLAR CELLS** ATTACHED TO ITS WINGS, WHICH STRETCH FOR 63.4 M

IT IS POWERED BY **FOUR ELECTRIC MOTORS**

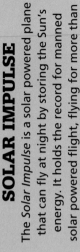

AIRBUS A340 TO SCALE

It has completed a trip of **2,500 KM** from **Europe** to **North Africa** in three stages and there are plans to fly it around the world in just **20 DAYS** without a drop of fuel.

BOEING 787 DREAMLINER

First flown in 2009, this passenger plane's windows are **65% larger** than other aircraft. The windows use dimmers instead of shades.

To make it, workers drilled only 10,000 holes into the fuselage, rather than 1 million in a superjumbo 747.

What is a 787 made from?

50%
LIGHTWEIGHT COMPOSITE MATERIALS

20%
ALUMINIUM

15%
TITANIUM

10%
STEEL

5%
OTHER MATERIALS

LONGEST NON-STOP PASSENGER FLIGHTS

JOHANNESBURG TO ATLANTA 17 HOURS

SINGAPORE TO NEWARK 18 HOURS

SINGAPORE TO LOS ANGELES 18 HOURS 30 MINUTES

DALLAS-FORT WORTH TO SYDNEY 18 HOURS 30 MINUTES

SKYLON

The proposed Skylon space plane will use a new type of engine, called SABRE. This works like a cross between a jet (in the low atmosphere) and a rocket (in the higher atmosphere) pushing it to a speed of

IT COULD CARRY SATELLITES INTO ORBIT.

MACH 25
(25 TIMES THE SPEED OF SOUND)

SPACE EXPLORATION

In order to learn more about space, we have built powerful telescopes that can peer billions of light years into space, and robot spacecraft to explore the outer reaches of the Solar System.

HUBBLE SPACE TELESCOPE

This space telescope orbits the Earth every 97 minutes at a speed of about 8 km per second. It can pass over the USA in just 10 minutes.

2.4 METRES

THE DIAMETER OF HUBBLE'S MAIN REFLECTING MIRROR – THAT IS TALLER THAN AN ADULT HUMAN.

120 GB

THE AMOUNT OF INFORMATION HUBBLE SENDS BACK TO EARTH EACH WEEK – ENOUGH TO FILL 25 DVDS.

DISTANCE TRAVELLED
These images show the total distances travelled by some of the world's most pioneering spacecraft. Some have reached the very edge of our Solar System.

APOLLO 11
THE FIRST MISSION TO LAND PEOPLE ON THE MOON IN 1969.

1.5 MILLION KM

SPUTNIK 1
THE FIRST ARTIFICIAL SATELLITE. IT WAS LAUNCHED ON 4 JANUARY 1958.

70 MILLION KM

1,400
The number of times Sputnik 1 orbited Earth in 1957 before it re-entered the atmosphere 92 days after its launch.

CASSINI
SPACE PROBE SENT TO SATURN IN 1997.

3.5 BILLION KM

1 BILLION KM

SPACECRAFT (TO SCALE)

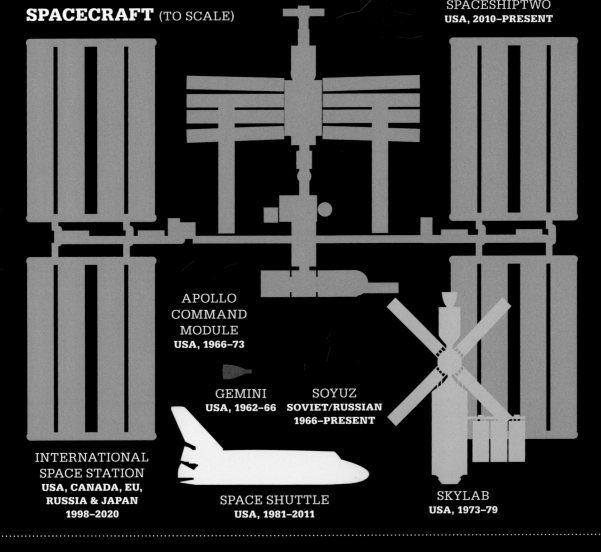

SPACESHIPTWO
USA, 2010–PRESENT

APOLLO COMMAND MODULE
USA, 1966–73

GEMINI
USA, 1962–66

SOYUZ
SOVIET/RUSSIAN
1966–PRESENT

INTERNATIONAL SPACE STATION
USA, CANADA, EU,
RUSSIA & JAPAN
1998–2020

SPACE SHUTTLE
USA, 1981–2011

SKYLAB
USA, 1973–79

VOYAGER 1
LAUNCHED IN 1977, VOYAGER 1 IS EXPECTED
TO BECOME THE FIRST MAN-MADE OBJECT
TO LEAVE THE SOLAR SYSTEM.

18.4 BILLION KM

VOYAGER 2
FLEW PAST SATURN, JUPITER,
URANUS AND NEPTUNE
AFTER ITS 1977 LAUNCH.

15 BILLION KM

17 HOURS
The time it takes for radio
signals travelling at the
speed of light to reach
Voyager 1 from Earth.

11 BILLION KM

20 BILLION KM

SCIENCE

In Europe, scientists have built the world's largest machine to study the Universe. At the other extreme, microscopic structures are being developed to form Earth's strongest materials.

100°C Boiling point of water

37 °C Human body temperature

0°C

LARGE HADRON COLLIDER

The Large Hadron Collider (LHC) is an enormous circular tunnel where tiny particles are sent crashing into each other at close to the speed of light. Scientists study the results of these collisions to learn more about how the Universe was formed and how it works.

FRANCE
LHC
SWITZERLAND

THE LHC TUNNEL IS **8.5 KM IN DIAMETER**

MANHATTAN, NEW YORK, USA 21.5 KM LONG

Protons race around the tunnel **11,245 times a second**

-89.2 °C Lowest recorded temperature on Earth

600 million collisions occur in the tunnel each second, generating temperatures **100,000** times hotter than the core of **the Sun.**

-210 °C Melting point of Nitrogen

The LHC uses **9,300 magnets** cooled to **-193°C** using **10,080 tonnes of liquid nitrogen.** The magnets are then cooled further to

-271.3°C

by liquid helium

-273.15 °C Absolute zero

Each year, the Large Hadron Collider produces enough data to fill **180,000** DVDs.

ROBOTS

The world's first production-line robot appeared in 1961. Called Unimate, it worked in a car factory where it moved and stacked red-hot metal parts.

San Francisco

Hawaii

Brisbane

In **December 2012**, a self-controlled robot completed a record-breaking **16,668 km** trip across the Pacific, from San Francisco to Australia.

NANOTECHNOLOGY

Nanotechnology deals with objects that are one billionth of a metre in size. Tiny nanotubes are used to produce lightweight but strong materials, including tiny electrical components.

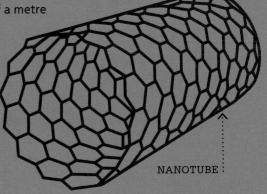

NANOTUBE

If a nanometre was blown up 10 million times, it would still only be the size of a **marble**, while a football increased by the same amount would be the size of the Moon.

EARTH SCIENCES

Scientists use the Moment Magnitude Scale to measure earthquakes. This graph shows how many earthquakes occur each year, their magnitude and their power.

EARTHQUAKE ENERGY EQUIVALENTS

MAGNITUDE

ENERGY RELEASE
KG OF EXPLOSIVES

Magnitude	Event	Energy Release
10		56,000,000,000,000
9	Chile **1960** / Japan **2011**	1,800,000,000,000
8	Largest nuclear test **1961** / Mexico **1985**	56,000,000,000
7	Iran **1780**	1,800,000,000
6	Hiroshima atomic bomb **1945**	56,000,000
5		1,800,000
4		56,000
3	Large lightning bolt	1,800
2		56

NUMBER OF EARTHQUAKES PER YEAR

1   15   150   1,500   10,000   100,000   1,000,000

MEDICINE AND HEALTH CARE

There are around 134 million births every year, compared to just 56 million deaths. And thanks to medical advances, many people are living longer than ever before, making the world's population grow very fast.

LONGER LIVES

Over the last 60 years, improvements in diet, health and medicine around the world have seen the average life expectancy rise.

Average worldwide life expectancy

45 YEARS — men
48 YEARS — women
65 YEARS — men
70 YEARS — women

1950   2010

GUATEMALA

The influenza pandemic of **1918–1919** killed more than **15 million people** around the world, more than the entire population of **Guatemala.**

Nearly **9 million children** under **5 years of age**, or 1.4 per cent of the world's under-5 population, die each year from conditions that could be treated with medicines.

SMALLPOX

Smallpox was a disease that once killed around 4 million people a year worldwide. In 1979, it was the first disease to be wiped out by vaccines.

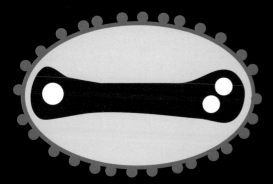

The disease was caused by a tiny virus, just 400 nanometres across – shown here 400 million times its actual size

 Smallpox historically killed **30%** of the people who caught it.

18th century
60,000,000
PEOPLE DIED FROM SMALLPOX IN EUROPE.

20th century
300,000,000
people killed by smallpox around the world.

 The last known case of smallpox occurred in **Somalia in 1977.**

TODAY, IT NO LONGER EXISTS NATURALLY.

DIPHTHERIA DEATHS IN THE UK
Before and after use of **vaccine**.

1940–1944
1,830 per year

1969
0

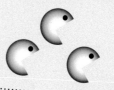

VACCINATION

A weak form of the disease germ is injected into the body.

The body makes antibodies that fight the germ.

Should the real disease germs ever attack the body, the antibodies will return and destroy them.

*ET: The Extra-
Terrestrial* (1982)

FILM

Thousands of movies are released every year, thrilling people with stories of excitement, love and adventure. The most successful films can earn more than a billion dollars.

Titanic (1997)

CHARACTERS WHO HAVE APPEARED IN THE MOST MOVIES

THE DEVIL
544 MOVIES

SANTA CLAUS
303 MOVIES

THE GRIM REAPER
290 MOVIES

Tootsie (1982)
Beverly Hills Cop (1984)

**MOST VEHICLES
DESTROYED IN A FILM**
*TRANSFORMERS: DARK
OF THE MOON* (2011)

JESUS CHRIST
239 MOVIES

GOD
231 MOVIES

HIGHEST-GROSSING FILMS
These movies smashed all records by taking the most money at cinemas around the world.

532

AVATAR (2009)
US$ 2.8 BILLION

TITANIC (1997)
US$ 2.2 BILLION

28 MOVIES

JAMES BOND
25 MOVIES

STAR TREK
FRIDAY THE 13TH
NATIONAL LAMPOON
12 MOVIES

BATMAN
PINK PANTHER
11 MOVIES

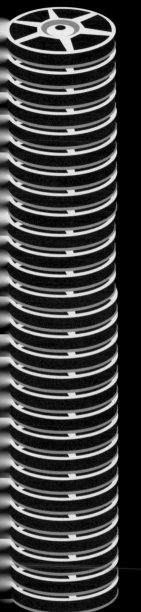

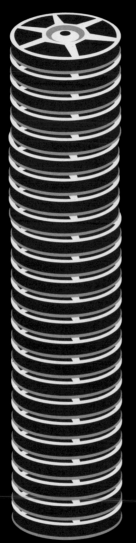

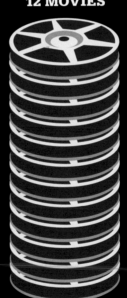

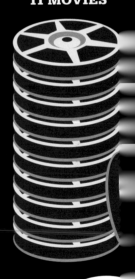

*MARVEL'S
THE AVENGERS
(2012)* **US$ 1.5 BILLION**

*HARRY POTTER
AND THE DEATHLY
HALLOWS PART 2* **(2011)
US$1.3 BILLION**

IRON MAN 3 **(2013)
US$1.2 BILLION**

Made fo
budget o
US$15,000, ho
Paranormal Ac
US$197 million
office – a retur
than 650,000

MOVIE STARS

Big movies need big stars. With films earning huge amounts of money, the biggest stars can earn US$20 million for every movie they make.

MR SPIELBERG

The highest-grossing director of all time is Steven Spielberg. As of 2012, his 30 movies had taken US$9.38 billion at the box office around the world.

HIGHEST-PAID ACTORS

This is what Hollywood's top stars were paid between **JUNE 2012 AND JUNE 2013**

**ROBERT DOWNEY JR
US$75 MILLION**

**CHANNING TATUM
US$60 MILLION**

**HUGH JACKMAN
US$55 MILLION**

**MARK WAHLBERG
US$52 MILLION**

HIGHEST-GROSSING MOVIE STARS

$ $

FRANK WELKER (97 MOVIES) US$6.45 BILLION

$ $

SAMUEL L JACKSON (84 MOVIES) US$5.15 BILLION

$ $ $ $ $ $ $ $ $ $ $ $ $ $ $ $ $ $ $ $

TOM HANKS (44 MOVIES) US$4.24 BILLION

$ $ $ $ $ $ $ $ $ $ $ $ $ $ $ $ $ $

JOHN RATZENBERGER (32 MOVIES) US$3.91 BILLION

$ $ $ $ $ $ $ $ $ $ $ $ $ $ $ $ $

EDDIE MURPHY (38 MOVIES) US$3.81 BILLION

FRANK WELKER

Frank Welker doesn't actually appear in his movies. Instead, he supplies voices for some of the most successful movies ever, including the Transformers series of films.

RIN TIN TIN

LASSIE

STRONGHEART

ANIMAL MOVIE STARS

Three dogs have stars on the Hollywood Walk of Fame. German Shepherd Rin Tin Tin starred in 20 films, while Strongheart was a movie star during the 1920s. Lassie is a character that has been portrayed on film and TV for more than 70 years and is in its 10th generation of dog actor.

DWAYNE JOHNSON
US$42 MILLION

LEONARDO DICAPRIO
US$39 MILLION

ADAM SANDLER
US$37 MILLION

Rin Tin Tin used to sign his movie contracts using his paw print.

127

TELEVISION

The first television broadcasts began more than 80 years ago in 1936. Today, billions of people around the world tune in every day to watch variety shows, cookery programmes and soap operas.

LONG-RUNNING TV SHOWS

Sábado Gigante
variety show, **Chile**

1962 over **2,000** episodes → **present**

1960 *Hasta La Cocina*, cookery show, **Mexico**

1956 *Guiding Light*, soap opera, **USA**

PANASONIC PRODUCE A
152-INCH
3-D HD-TV
WHICH MEASURES
3.4 M WIDE AND 1.8 M HIGH.

THE SMALLEST TV SCREEN, BUILT BY MICROEMISSIVE, MEASURES JUST **3.84 x 2.88 MM** WITH A RESOLUTION OF 160 X 120 PIXELS – IT'S SMALLER THAN YOUR FINGERNAIL.

■ ⟵···· **ACTUAL SIZE**

THE BIGGEST GAME SHOW WINNINGS
€3.5 MILLION

won by Bernd Stadelman on German Pro 7 show *Beat the Raab* in 2012.

The world's first TV advert appeared on **1 JULY 1941** for the Bulova Watch Company. The company paid **US$9.**

February 2012

Mon	Tue	Wed	Thu	Fri	Sat	Sun
30	31	1	2	3	4	5
6	7	8	9	10	11	12
13	14	15	16	17	18	19
20	21	22	23	24	25	26
27	28	29	1	2	3	4

Jeremiah Franco and Carin Shreve set the record for TV watching when they completed **86 hours 37 minutes** watching back-to-back *Simpsons* episodes from 8–12 February 2012.

more than **11,500** episodes   **present**

over **15,000** episodes **2009**

MOST EXPENSIVE TV SERIES

WHERE THE MONEY GOES

Locations

Actors

Special Effects

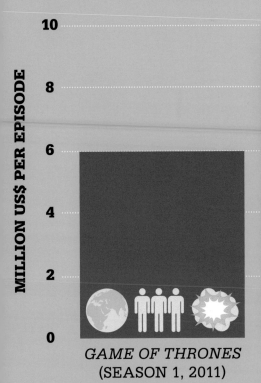

MILLION US$ PER EPISODE

GAME OF THRONES (SEASON 1, 2011)

FRIENDS (FINAL SERIES, 2003)

TERRA NOVA (SEASON 1, 2011)

129

THE STAGE

Plays have been performed for more than 2,500 years and are still one of the most popular forms of entertainment. Every year, some 13 million people go to a theatre in the UK alone.

The world's oldest theatre was the **THEATRE OF DIONYSIUS** in Athens. Built around 500 BCE, it could seat **17,000** people.

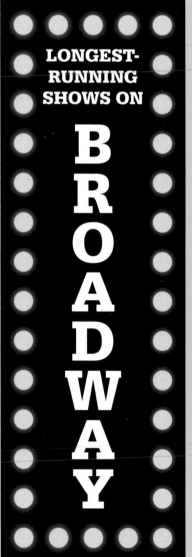

LONGEST-RUNNING SHOWS ON **BROADWAY**

PHANTOM OF THE OPERA **10,799** SHOWS

CATS **7,485** SHOWS

CHICAGO **7,125** SHOWS

THE LION KING **6,718** SHOWS

LES MISÉRABLES **6,325** SHOWS

as of January 2014

Actors should never whistle on stage. This belief dates back to old theatre riggers who used to communicate using whistles and could get confused.

SHORTEST AND LONGEST

35 seconds

The shortest play is *Breath* by Samuel Beckett. It is **35 seconds** long and has no actors – just sound effects and lighting changes. In contrast, *The Warp* by Neil Oram last for a total of **22 hours**. It is actually 10 individual shorter plays that are usually performed in one stage marathon.

The **biggest** theatre in the world today is the **Great Auditorium**, part of the Great Hall of the People in Tiananmen Square, **Beijing**, China. It can seat **10,000 people.**

THE WORLD'S **LONGEST RUNNING PLAY** IS *THE MOUSETRAP* by Dame Agatha Christie.

60 YEARS

SHAKESPEARE FACTS

He was responsible for 1,700 words we use every day, including *aerial, submerge, reliance, exposure, assassination* as well as several common phrases, including **break the ice it's all Greek to me one fell swoop**

HE WROTE AT LEAST

37 PLAYS

ONE OF WHICH, *CARDENIO*, IS LOST. THE FIRST, *LOVE'S LABOUR'S LOST*, WAS WRITTEN IN 1588–97 AND THE LAST, *HENRY VIII*, WAS WRITTEN IN 1613.

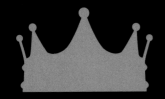

It is considered bad luck to wish someone "good luck" in a theatre. Instead, actors may wish each other to **"BREAK A LEG".**

THEATRE SUPERSTITIONS

Actors believe you should never refer to Shakespeare's play *Macbeth* by its name. Instead, they call it **"THE SCOTTISH PLAY".**

AWARDS

Outstanding achievements in film and TV are often recognised with awards at glamorous ceremonies. Categories include acting and directing, as well as costume design and special effects. There are also awards for some of the worst shows and performances.

THE ACADEMY AWARDS

Academy Awards, or Oscars, are awarded for special achievements in movies. Categories include best actor and actress and best film.

4

Katharine Hepburn has won more Oscars than any other actor or actress. She has won four best actress Oscars.

Three films hold the record for the most Oscar wins with 11 – *Ben Hur* (1959), *Titanic* (1997) and *The Return of the King* (2003).

11

THE RETURN OF THE KING IS THE ONLY MOVIE TO WIN ALL THE OSCARS IT WAS NOMINATED FOR.

22

Walt Disney has personally won more Oscars than anyone else. He was nominated 59 times and won 22.

AN **OSCAR** WEIGHS JUST OVER **3 KG** AND IS **34 CM** TALL.

THE BAFTA AWARDS

The British Academy of Film and Television Arts gives awards for TV and movies.

Film director **Woody Allen** has won eight awards for his movies, such as *Annie Hall*.

THE OLIVIER AWARDS

The Laurence Olivier Awards are presented for achievements in British theatre.

The Curious Incident of the Dog in the Night-Time shares the record for the most awards in one year, winning seven in 2013. The musical *Matilda* won seven in 2012.

THE EMMY AWARDS

Awarded for achievements on US television

AN **EMMY** WEIGHS JUST OVER **3 KG** AND IS **39 CM** TALL.

8

Most Emmys won by a female performer: **Cloris Leachman**.

7

Most Emmys won by a male performer: **Edward Asner**.

Most Emmys won by a series: *Frasier*.

37

THE RAZZIES

The Golden Raspberry, or Razzie, is awarded to bad films and performances.

Adam Sandler holds the record for winning the most with **11 Razzies**.

BOOKS

Books come in all sizes, from the gigantic to the microscopic. Today, the development of e-books means that you can carry an entire library of books in the palm of your hand.

FIVE LONGEST NOVELS IN THE ENGLISH LANGUAGE

SIRONIA, TEXAS
MADISON COOPER
1952

POOR FELLOW MY COUNTRY
XAVIER HERBERT
1975

1.2 MILLION WORDS

1.1 MILLION WORDS

969,000 WORDS

850,000 WORDS

700,000 WORDS

MISSION EARTH
L. RON HUBBARD
1985

CLARISSA
SAMUEL RICHARDSON
1748

MISS MACINTOSH, MY DARLING
MARGUERITE YOUNG
1965

MOST EXPENSIVE BOOK

THE CODEX LEICESTER
Leonardo da Vinci
(c. 1510)
US$30.8 MILLION

The most expensive book ever sold, *The Codex Leicester*, is a 32-page document that was written in 1506–1510 by Leonardo da Vinci.

It was written in Leonardo's distinctive mirror writing

BACKWARDS!

THE ST CUTHBERT GOSPEL
(c. 650)
US$14.1 MILLION

THE GOSPELS OF HENRY THE LION
Order of St Benedict
(c. 1175)
US$11.7 MILLION

BIRDS OF AMERICA
James Audubon
(c. 1830)
US$11.5 MILLION

THE CANTERBURY TALES Geoffrey Chaucer (c. 1400)
US$7.5 MILLION

Made in 2007, the world's smallest book measures just **0.07 x 0.1 mm** – smaller than the full stop at the end of this sentence. It is *Teeny Ted from Turnip Town* and each page was carved onto silicon using a laser. It can only be read using a powerful microscope.

THE BIGGEST LIBRARY IN THE WORLD

151.8 MILLION ITEMS, INCLUDING **34.5 MILLION BOOKS** AND OTHER PRINTED MATERIALS IN **470 LANGUAGES**

EMPLOYS **3,525** PERMANENT MEMBERS OF STAFF

1,380 KM OF BOOKSHELVES

1.7 MILLION VISITORS EVERY YEAR

1,004,725

approximate number of books published around the world each year.

ONE OF THE WORLD'S LARGEST BOOKS IS THE KLENCKE ATLAS, WHICH MEASURES 1.75 X 1.9 M. IT IS 350 YEARS OLD...

... AND TAKES SIX PEOPLE TO LIFT IT.

RISE OF THE E-BOOK
US e-book sales

2002	2006	2010	2012
US$2.1 MILLION	US$25.2 MILLION	US$441.3 MILLION	US$621.3 MILLION

135

COMICS

Since the first comic book was published in 1837, cartoon strips have created invincible super-heroes and action-packed adventures that have even made it onto the big screen.

Comic timeline

First appearance of super-heroes

First appearance of comic strips

WONDER WOMAN
All Star Comics #8

CAPTAIN AMERICA
Captain America Comics #1

SUPERMAN
Action Comics #1

1941

1938

BRENDA STARR

1940

BLONDIE

1930

1918

1897

GASOLINE ALLEY

THE KATZENJAMMER KIDS

1924

ANNIE

1930

DICK TRACY

1937

PRINCE VALIANT

1939

BATMAN
Detective Comics #27

THE LARGEST GRAPHIC NOVEL
Romeo and Juliet: The War by Stan Lee. A limited collector's edition measured

FIRST COMIC SUPERHERO
THE PHANTOM, CREATED BY LEE FALK IN 1936

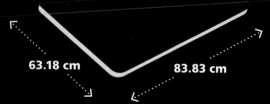

63.18 cm   83.83 cm

Just 25 copies were printed.

COMIC BOOK CONVENTIONS
Comic-Con in the USA attracts some **125,000.** The busiest comic festival is Japan's **Comiket.** In 2012 **560,000** visited the festival.

THE LONGEST COMIC STRIP

Drawn by French students in 2011, the longest comic strip measured more than 1,000 m long – enough to wrap around a football pitch more than three times.

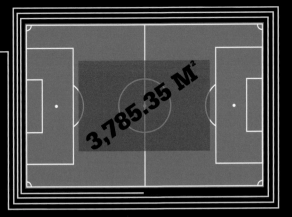

3,785.35 M²

THE LARGEST COMIC STRIP

Drawn in Japan in 2010 and made up of 13 panels, with each panel showing a player from the Japanese football team. It measured 3,785.35 m² – more than half a football pitch.

DENNIS THE MENACE

1951

1963

THE AVENGERS
The Avengers #1

FIRST GRAPHIC NOVEL
BLOODSTAR
BY RICHARD CORBEN
(1976)

1950

1958

1962

BEETLE BAILEY

B.C.

SPIDERMAN
Amazing Fantasy #15

Since it was first printed in 1950, the comic strip *Peanuts* has appeared in more than

2,500 newspapers around the world,

and read by some

355,000,000 people.

In 2010, a copy of the 1938 comic in which Superman first appeared
ACTION COMICS #1
sold for **US$2.16 MILLION**
The original cover price was
10 cents.
To buy it in 2010, you would have needed a stack of 10 cent coins 29 km tall – more than three times the height of Everest.

10c

1938

2010

MUSIC

Musical pieces can be long operas or even short periods of silence, while the groups that play them can contain thousands of instrument players and singers.

4'33" BY JOHN CAGE

The piece involves a pianist sitting at a piano for four minutes and 33 seconds without playing a single note.

1,000 YEARS

The length of time it would take to perform *The Longplayer* by Jem Finer. The piece is being played out by computers at listening posts in the UK, USA, Egypt and Australia and will not finish until the year 2999.

LONG OPERAS

THE HERETICS
GABRIEL VON WAYDITCH
8 HOURS 30 MINUTES

THE LIFE AND TIMES OF JOSEPH STALIN
ROBERT WILSON
13 HOURS 25 MINUTES

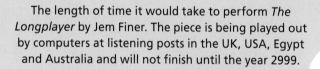

LARGEST CHOIR
121,440
singers assembled in January 2011 at Perugalathur, India.

THE WORLD'S LARGEST VIOLIN

Built by 15 skilled workers, the world's largest violin is

4.27 M LONG

and takes three musicians to play.

MOST EXPENSIVE MUSICAL INSTRUMENT

A Stradivarius violin, called the Lady Blunt, was sold for

US$15.9 MILLION

in 2011 to raise money for the Japanese Tsunami Relief Fund.

ORCHESTRA

How the instruments in an orchestra are arranged.

WOODWIND
STRINGS
BRASS
PERCUSSION

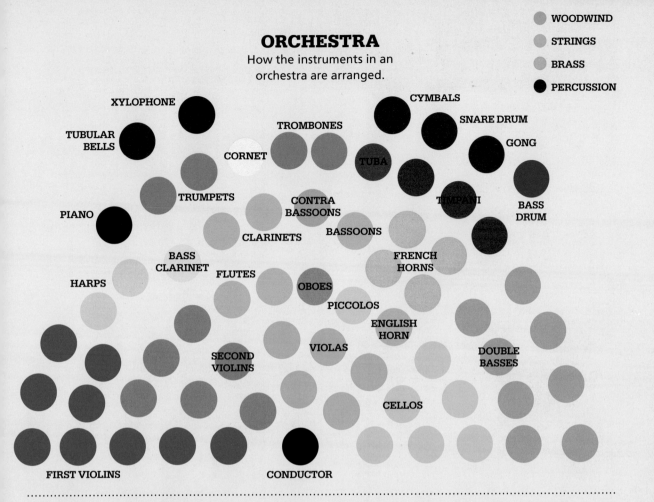

XYLOPHONE
TUBULAR BELLS
CORNET
TROMBONES
CYMBALS
SNARE DRUM
GONG
TUBA
TRUMPETS
CONTRA BASSOONS
TIMPANI
BASS DRUM
PIANO
CLARINETS
BASSOONS
BASS CLARINET
FLUTES
OBOES
FRENCH HORNS
HARPS
PICCOLOS
ENGLISH HORN
SECOND VIOLINS
VIOLAS
DOUBLE BASSES
CELLOS
FIRST VIOLINS
CONDUCTOR

In 1998, nearly

4,000

children formed an enormous orchestra to play Sir Malcolm Arnold's *Little Suite No 2*. The orchestra included **1,600 string players**, **1,300 woodwind**, **800 brass** and more than **200 percussion**.

MUSICAL SYMBOLS

Musicians use various symbols to show the notes of a piece of music. This is called musical notation.

BASS CLEF
BREVE
MINIM
QUAVER
ALTO CLEF
SEMIBREVE
CROTCHET
SEMIQUAVER
TREBLE CLEF

ROCK AND POP

Sales of rock and pop music have earned performers millions of dollars and turned them into global superstars.

BIGGEST SELLING ALBUMS OF ALL TIME

THRILLER **(1982)**
MICHAEL JACKSON
65 MILLION

THE DARK SIDE OF THE MOON **(1973)**
PINK FLOYD
50 MILLION

THE GRAMMY AWARDS

The Grammys are awarded by the National Academy of Recording Arts and Sciences of the United States for achievements in the recording industry.

8

Michael Jackson (1984) and **Santana** (2000) hold the record for winning the most grammys in a single year, with eight.

The best-selling single of all time

50,000,000

WHITE CHRISTMAS (1942)
BING CROSBY

Longest gig

Rock musician Bruce Springsteen played a concert on 31 July 2012 in Helsinki, Finland, that lasted four hours and six minutes, breaking his own record for the longest gig.

DIGITAL 50.5%

DIGITAL VS PHYSICAL

In 2011, digital music sales in the US overtook physical sales (CDs and records) for the first time, making up 50.5% of all sales.

PHYSICAL 49.5%

BACK IN BLACK **(1980)**
AC/DC
49 MILLION

THE BODYGUARD **(1992)**
WHITNEY HOUSTON/VARIOUS
44 MILLION

BAT OUT OF HELL **(1977)**
MEAT LOAF
43 MILLION

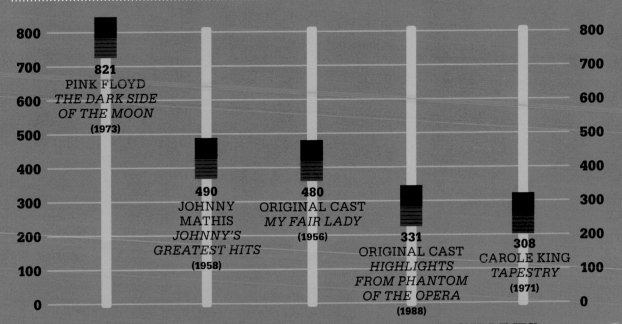

821
PINK FLOYD
THE DARK SIDE OF THE MOON
(1973)

490
JOHNNY MATHIS
JOHNNY'S GREATEST HITS
(1958)

480
ORIGINAL CAST
MY FAIR LADY
(1956)

331
ORIGINAL CAST
HIGHLIGHTS FROM PHANTOM OF THE OPERA
(1988)

308
CAROLE KING
TAPESTRY
(1971)

MOST WEEKS IN THE US BILLBOARD CHARTS
(as of January 2013)

PLAYTIME

Toys and games aren't just for kids! Super-sized and super-expensive versions of classic play things have broken world records and become global sensations.

RUBIK'S CUBE

 The puzzle was invented in **1974** by Hungarian professor Ernö Rubik.

 More than **300 million** have been sold around the world.

 In March 2013, Mats Valk solved a cube in just **5.5 seconds.**

BIGGEST RUBIK'S CUBE WEIGHS MORE THAN
500 KG
OR SEVEN ADULT MALES

3 METRES

BIGGEST SKATEBOARD

The world's biggest skateboard weighs more than 1,600 kg and is
11.14 M LONG

Some of the **oldest toys** have been found in the remains of **ancient Sumer** and date back to **2600** BCE. They are simple figures of people and animals.

CHESS

Chess is one of the oldest board games in the world. It first appeared in India in the 6th century CE.

The world's most expensive chess set has pieces made of gold and platinum and studded with rubies, emeralds and diamonds. It's value is

US$9.8 MILLION

A TEDDY BEAR MADE BY GERMAN COMPANY STEIFF, SOLD FOR A RECORD
US$171,600 AT AUCTION IN 1994.

More than **275 million** Monopoly sets have been sold in **111** countries and **43** languages.

40 billion LEGO bricks stacked together would reach the Moon.

36 BILLION

The number of LEGO bricks produced each year. That is 68,000 every single minute.

143

GAMING

While the first video games were made up of simple dots
lines, today's gamers can play super-realistic games and
compete with people on the other side of the world.

LARGEST WORKING GAMES CONTROLLER

3.6 METRES

A massive NES Games controller weighing
20 kg was built in 2012 by engineering students
from TU Delft University, Netherlands.

CHRIS MCGIVERN
FROM THE UK SPENT

20 HOURS
24 MINUTES
43 SECONDS

SETTING A DANCE
GAME MARATHON
RECORD IN 2011
PLAYING *DANCE
DANCE REVOLUTION*

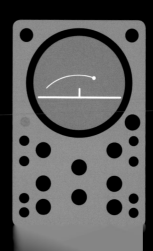

GROWTH OF THE VIDEO GAMES INDUSTRY

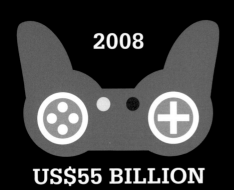

2008

US$55 BILLION

2012

US$68 BILLION

In comparison, the movie industry was only worth US$32 billion in 2012.

POPULAR GAMES CONSOLES (IN UNITS SOLD)

Nintendo DS 153 million

Wii 99 million

Xbox 76 million

PlayStation 70 million

SOCIAL GAMING

Social network game *CityVille* managed to collect 26 million online players within 12 days of its launch. That is more people than the population of Australia.

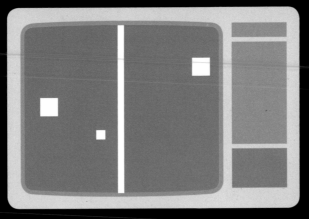

THE FIRST HOME VIDEO GAMES CONSOLE

Magnavox Odyssey launched in 1972 with simple line and dot games, such as *Pong*.

PAINTING AND PHOTOGRAPHY

Works of art can be created on any surface, including canvas, paper and glass. The best examples will sell for millions of dollars – even if they are painted onto the sides of buildings!

The world's most expensive photograph is *Rhine II* taken by Andreas Gursky from Germany. In 2011, it was sold for US$4.3 million.

PABLO PICASSO

is recognised as the most prolific painter ever. During his career of 75 years, he produced

100,000
PRINTS AND ENGRAVINGS

34,000
BOOK ILLUSTRATIONS

13,500
PAINTINGS

300
SCULPTURES AND CERAMICS

That is a rate of more than five works of art every single day.

The **frescoes** on the ceiling of the **Sistine Chapel** took Michelangelo **four years** to complete (1508–1512). The Chapel itself is 40.23 m long and 13.4 m wide.

MOST EXPENSIVE WORKS OF ART

US$250 MILLION

The Card Players, **1893**
Paul Cézanne

US$140 MILLION

No.5, 1948, **1948**
Jackson Pollock

US$137.5 MILLION

Woman III, **1953**
Willem de Kooning

US$135 MILLION

Portrait of Adele Bloch-Bauer, **1907**
Gustav Klimt

US$119.9 MILLION

The Scream, **1885**
Edvard Munch

LONGEST PAINTING MEASURES 6,000 M LONG AND WAS PAINTED BY 3,000 SCHOOL STUDENTS FROM MEXICO.

The Hermitage Museum
(St Petersburg, Russia), has more than

**2.7 MILLION EXHIBITS,
24 KM OF GALLERIES,
1,786 DOORS, 1,945 WINDOWS AND
1,057 HALLS AND ROOMS.**

In 1997, street artist Saber created an enormous piece of graffiti. Painted on the concrete banks of the Los Angeles River it needed more than 350 litres of paint and took the artist 35 nights to complete.

Perhaps the most famous painting in the World is the *Mona Lisa* (or *La Gioconda*) by **Leonardo da Vinci**. It hangs in the Musée du Louvre in Paris, France, and measures 77 x 53 cm.

SCULPTURE AND INSTALLATION

Some of the biggest art works of all, installations and statues can cover enormous areas and rise tens of metres into the sky.

Artists Christo and Jeanne-Claude are well-known for creating huge works of art. In 1991, they installed

3,100

umbrellas in long chains across valleys in Japan and the USA. The Japan chain measured

19 km long,

while the US chain measured

29 km long.

Their *Surrounded Islands* project from 1983 saw them use

603,870 sq m of bright pink plastic

to wrap around the coasts of 11 islands in Biscayne Bay near Miami, Florida, USA.

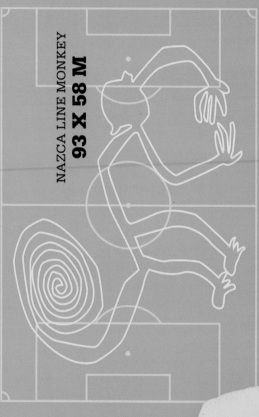

NAZCA LINE MONKEY
93 X 58 M

FOOTBALL PITCH 105 X 68 M

NAZCA LINES

These are huge line drawings made on the desert floor of Peru. They stretch over an area of 500 sq km and were made more than 2,000 years ago. They show plants and animals, and individual pictures are up to 235 m long.

BIG STATUES

Here are some of the world's tallest statues, with their heights.

SPRING TEMPLE BUDDHA

LUSHAN, HENAN, CHINA

128 M

LARGEST MODELLING BALLOON SCULPTURE

A spider measuring 6.76 m across and made from 2,975 balloons was installed in a waterpark in Grand Mound, Washington, USA in 2011.

THE MOTHERLAND CALLS
MAMAYEV, RUSSIA
85 M

In 1917, French artist Marcel Duchamp made art history when he took a urinal and turned it into a work of art by laying it on its back and calling it *Fountain*.

CHRIST THE REDEEMER
RIO DE JANEIRO, BRAZIL
39.6 M

STATUE OF LIBERTY
NEW YORK, USA
93 M

RUNNING AND JUMPING

These intense sports push competitors to their limits. Runners compete over distances ranging from 100 metres to the 42-km-long marathon – a real test of endurance.

FASTER AND FASTER

Over the last 100 years, the record for the men's 100 metres has decreased by more than a second. In the same period, the women's 100 metres record has decreased from 13.6 seconds to 10.49 seconds. The men's world record for the wheelchair 100 metres is 13.63 seconds.

2009 USAIN BOLT (JAMAICA)

2008 USAIN BOLT (JAMAICA)

1999 MAURICE GREENE (USA)

1991 CARL LEWIS (USA)

1968 JIM HINES (USA)

1964 BOB HAYES (USA)

1912 DONALD LIPPINCOTT (USA)

WHITE = GOOD JUMP

RED = FOUL

FLAGS USED BY JUDGES FOR JUMPING COMPETITIONS

LONG JUMP V TRIPLE JUMP

The men's long jump record is nearly the length of a school bus. For the triple jump, athletes first take a long hop, then a step, before trying to jump as far as they can. All three elements are added together to give the length of the athlete's attempt.

LONG JUMP RECORD (WOMEN'S)
GALINA CHRISTYAKOVA
(USSR) 1988
7.52 m

LONG JUMP RECORD (MEN'S)
MIKE POWELL
(USA) 1991
8.95 m

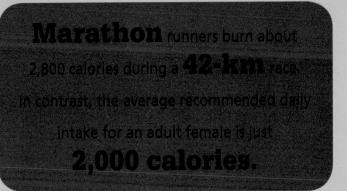

Marathon runners burn about 2,800 calories during a **42-km** race. In contrast, the average recommended daily intake for an adult female is just **2,000 calories.**

9.58 SECONDS

9.69 SECONDS

9.79 SECONDS

9.86 SECONDS

9.95 SECONDS

10.06 SECONDS

10.60 SECONDS

VAULTING HIGH
Pole vault record – Sergei Bubka (Ukraine) 1994
6.14 m
– HIGHER THAN A GIRAFFE.

A red kangaroo bounds along in jumps that cover about 8 metres in a single leap, but some have been recorded covering 13 metres.

13 m

TRIPLE JUMP RECORD (WOMEN'S) INESSA KRAVETS (UKRAINE) 1995
15.50 m

TRIPLE JUMP RECORD (MEN'S) JONATHAN EDWARDS (UK) 1995
18.29 m

LIFTING AND THROWING

Lifting and throwing competitions involve amazing feats of explosive strength. A sudden surge of power is needed to lift the heaviest weights or throw an object the farthest.

Hossein Rezazadeh (Iran) holds the combined record for the snatch (lifting a weight above the head in one movement)

212.5 KG

and the clean and jerk (lifting a weight above the head in two movements)

260 KG

with the combined weight of

472.5 KG

THE SNATCH

THE CLEAN AND JERK

THE SAME WEIGHT AS 6.5 ADULTS!

23.12 m
SHOT PUT
RANDY BARNES (USA)
20 MAY 1990

THROWING RECORDS

The centre of an athletics arena sees athletes take part in throwing competitions using a wide range of equipment. These include the shot put, the hammer, the discus and the javelin.

CLUB THROW

The club throw is one of four throwing events at the Summer Paralympics. Athletes compete to see who can hurl a wooden club with a metal base the farthest. The club weighs 0.5 kg.

HAMMER

The hammer is not a hammer at all, but a heavy ball on the end of steel wire. The thrower usually spins around three to four times before releasing the hammer. It must land within a 35 degree area to record a successful throw.

METAL BASE

SAFETY CAGE

35 DEGREE AREA

THROWING CIRCLE

In 1986, the design of the javelin was altered to make throws **10 per cent shorter**. This was because athletes were starting to throw farther than many stadiums could hold – **sometimes in excess of**

100 METRES.

105 m
FOOTBALL PITCH (APPROX)

74.08 m
JÜRGEN SCHULT (E GERMANY)
DISCUS
6 JUNE 1986

86.74 m
YURIY SEDYKH (USSR)
HAMMER
30 AUGUST 1986

98.48 m
25 MAY 1996
JAN ZELEZNY (CZE)
JAVELIN
(NEW 1986 MODEL)

THE OLYMPICS

The Summer and Winter Olympics are held every four years. Thousands of athletes from around the world gather in the host city to take part in sports, competing to win gold, silver or bronze medals.

THE START

The Olympic Games of ancient Greece started in 776 BCE, and continued for more than 1,000 years before ending about 393 CE. It was another 1,500 years before the Games were held again, with the start of the modern Olympics at Athens in 1896.

THE MODERN SUMMER OLYMPICS

ATHENS 1896
NEARLY 280 ATHLETES
FROM 12 COUNTRIES

LONDON 2012
10,490 ATHLETES
FROM 204 COUNTRIES

THE SUMMER PARALYMPICS

ROME 1960
400 ATHLETES
FROM 23 COUNTRIES

LONDON 2012
4,200 ATHLETES
FROM 160 COUNTRIES

The most successful Olympian ever is swimmer Michael Phelps who has won 22 medals.

OLYMPIC TORCH

CARRIED BY SOME
8,000
TORCH BEARERS ON A
70-DAY
JOURNEY FROM GREECE TO LONDON COVERING
13,000 KM
OR THE EQUIVALENT OF MORE THAN ONE QUARTER OF THE WAY AROUND THE WORLD

18 GOLD, 2 SILVER, 2 BRONZE

	Gold	**Silver**	**Bronze**
NORWAY	107	106	90
USA	87	95	71
SOVIET UNION	78	57	59

Most successful countries at the Winter Olympics

There have been 21 Games since the first Winter Olympics was held in Chamonix in 1924. Medals are awarded in each event, with the winner taking the gold medal, the second-placed athlete the silver and the third-placed athlete the bronze.

OLYMPIC GOLDS PER HEAD OF POPULATION AT LONDON 2012

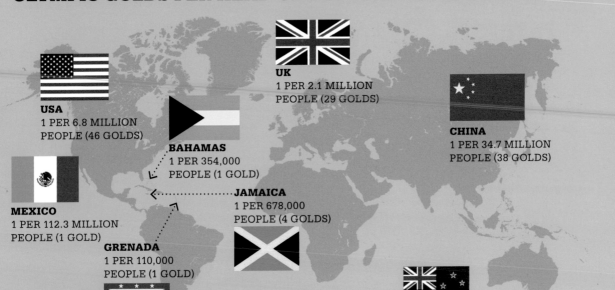

USA
1 PER 6.8 MILLION
PEOPLE (46 GOLDS)

BAHAMAS
1 PER 354,000
PEOPLE (1 GOLD)

MEXICO
1 PER 112.3 MILLION
PEOPLE (1 GOLD)

JAMAICA
1 PER 678,000
PEOPLE (4 GOLDS)

GRENADA
1 PER 110,000
PEOPLE (1 GOLD)

UK
1 PER 2.1 MILLION
PEOPLE (29 GOLDS)

CHINA
1 PER 34.7 MILLION
PEOPLE (38 GOLDS)

NEW ZEALAND
1 PER 739,000
PEOPLE (6 GOLDS)

TEAM SPORTS

The most popular sports in the world are team sports. They attract both the greatest number of players and the most spectators. Some teams are also worth huge sums of money.

NUMBER OF PLAYERS ON THE PITCH

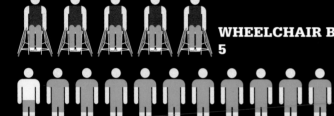

WHEELCHAIR BASKETBALL
5

FOOTBALL
11

AMERICAN FOOTBALL
11

RUGBY LEAGUE
13

RUGBY UNION
15

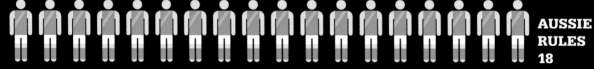

AUSSIE RULES
18

250 MILLION

The number of people playing football around the world. There are also an estimated

3.5 BILLION

football fans, making it the planet's most popular sport.

SCRUM V SCRIMMAGE

How teams line up to re-start a game

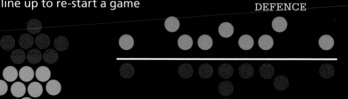

DEFENCE

OFFENCE

RUGBY UNION
SCRUM

AMERICAN FOOTBALL
SCRIMMAGE

HIGHEST SCORE IN
INTERNATIONAL FOOTBALL

0
American Samoa

31
Australia

LONGEST FIELD GOAL IN AMERICAN FOOTBALL

THE NFL
63 YDS

David Akers
San Francisco 49ers 2012
Sebastian Janikowski
Oakland Raiders 2011
Jason Elam
Denver Broncos 1998
Tom Dempsey
New Orleans Saints 1970

ALL-TIME
69 YDS

Ove Johansson
who made a 69 yard field goal while at Abilene Christian University in 1976.

120 YARDS LONG

53.3 YARDS WIDE

Most International Championships Won by Football Teams

EUROPEAN CHAMPIONSHIPS
GERMANY 3, SPAIN AND FRANCE 2

WORLD CUP
BRAZIL 5, ITALY 4, GERMANY 3

COPA AMÉRICAS
URUGUAY 15, ARGENTINA 14, BRAZIL 8

AFRICA CUP OF NATIONS
EGYPT 7, GHANA AND CAMEROON 4

MOST VALUABLE SPORTS TEAMS

- Manchester United (football – UK) – US$1.86 billion
- Dallas Cowboys (American football – USA) – US$1.81 billion
- New York Yankees (baseball – USA) – US$1.7 billion
- Washington Redskins (American football – USA) – US$1.55 billion
- Real Madrid (football – Spain) – US$1.45 billion

BASKETBALL

The Chicago Bulls hold the record for the most wins in a season with 72 wins (10 losses) in 1995–1996. The record for the most losses in a season is held by the Philadelphia 76ers with 73 losses (9 wins) in 1972–1973.

BATS AND BALLS

In these sports, the players have to try and hit a ball that may be travelling at more than 160 km/h – that is faster than cars are allowed to travel in most countries.

FASTEST

BASEBALL PITCH
162.3 KM/H
LYNN NOLAN RYAN
CALIFORNIA ANGELS
20 AUGUST 1974

CIRCUMFERENCE
229–235 mm

SEAM
Stitches two figure-of-eight pieces together

MATERIAL
String wrapped around a core of cork or rubber, covered in leather

WEIGHT
142–149 grammes

CRICKET DELIVERY
161.3 KM/H
SHOAIB AKHTAR
PAKISTAN
22 FEBRUARY 2003

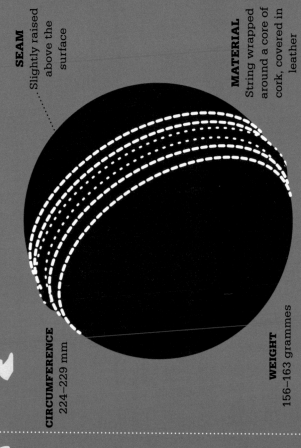

SEAM
Slightly raised above the surface

MATERIAL
String wrapped around a core of cork, covered in leather

CIRCUMFERENCE
224–229 mm

WEIGHT
156–163 grammes

CRICKET PITCH

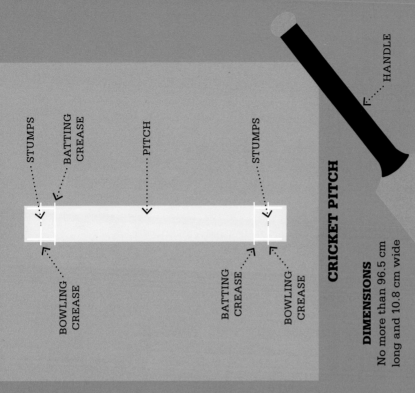

STUMPS

BATTING CREASE

PITCH

STUMPS

BOWLING CREASE

BATTING CREASE

BOWLING CREASE

HANDLE

WEIGHT
1.1–1.4 kg

DIMENSIONS
No more than 96.5 cm
long and 10.8 cm wide

MATERIAL
Sprung handle
spliced into a
wooden blade

BLADE

MOST SUCCESSFUL TEAM
ONE-DAY WORLD CUPS
AUSTRALIA WITH 4
(1987, 1999, 2003, 2007)

BASEBALL DIAMOND

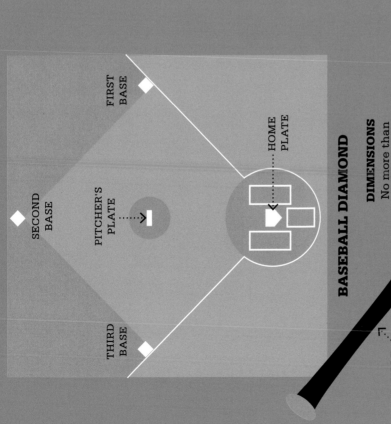

FIRST BASE

SECOND BASE

PITCHER'S PLATE

HOME PLATE

THIRD BASE

DIMENSIONS
No more than
107 cm long and
6.6 cm in diameter

WEIGHT
Usually no more than
0.94 kg, but there is
no maximum weight

BARREL

HANDLE

MATERIAL
One piece of solid
wood in Major
League Baseball

MOST SUCCESSFUL TEAM
WORLD SERIES TITLES
NEW YORK YANKEES WITH 27

SPORT ON WHEELS

These sports see who can go the fastest or travel the farthest. Today, the quickest wheeled vehicle can travel at more than 1,200 km/h.

MICHAEL SCHUMACHER GERMANY 7

JUAN MANUEL FANGIO ARGENTINA 5

ALAIN PROST FRANCE 4

RACE FLAGS

These are used to communicate between officials and drivers.

Chequered
Race or session has ended

Red
Race or session has been stopped

Yellow
Danger ahead

Green
All clear

Black flag with orange circle
Driver must return to the pits

White
Slow-moving vehicle

Blue
Warns drivers they are about to be lapped

Yellow and red striped
Slippery track ahead

Black/White
Warning of unsporting behaviour

Black flag
Driver has been disqualified

MOST FORMULA 1 CHAMPIONSHIPS

Each year, Formula 1 drivers compete to see who can win the most points over a season and win the drivers' championship. Points are awarded to drivers depending on where they finish each race, with the winner getting the most points.

TOP SPEEDS

The fastest motor sport is drag racing. The fastest cars use a special type of fuel, and are known as Top Fuel dragsters.

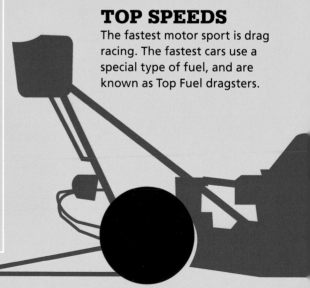

80 KM/H

The speed track cyclists can reach when racing around a **velodrome**.

Racing bike facts

Velodrome racing bikes have special adaptations that make them much faster than normal bikes.

With a frame made of superlight carbon fibre, the whole bike weighs less than 7 kg.

There is only one gear, so the bike can whizz round the track as quickly as possible.

Race bikes do not have brakes – the only way to slow down is to stop pedalling.

114.3 CM
HIGHEST OLLIE ON A SKATEBOARD
BY ALDRIN GARCIA, USA, 2011

LONG-DISTANCE CYCLING

Thomas Godwin (UK) holds the record for the greatest distance cycled in a year. In 1939, he managed 120,805 km – more than three times around the globe.

FORMULA 1 CAR
380 KM/H

TOP FUEL DRAGSTER
543.16 KM/H
TONY SCHUMACHER, USA 2005

IN THE WATER

Water sports are not all about speed. Sometimes, athletes compete to see who can perform with the most style – even when diving from heights of more than 27 metres.

DIVING

Jumping from a 10-metre board, an Olympic diver will hit the water at about

50 KM/H.

SWIMMING STROKES

Swimmers use four different strokes in competitions. These are front crawl (freestyle), back stroke, breast stroke and butterfly.

FRONT CRAWL

BACK STROKE

BREAST STROKE

BUTTERFLY

10 M
PLATFORM

3 M
SPRINGBOARD

1 M
SPRINGBOARD

75.2 M

FASTEST SAILING AROUND THE WORLD

45 DAYS
13 HOURS
42 MINUTES

THE FRENCH TRIMARAN
BANQUE POPULAIRE V
IN 2011.

Start/Finish: France

Atlantic Ocean

Pacific Ocean

Indian Ocean

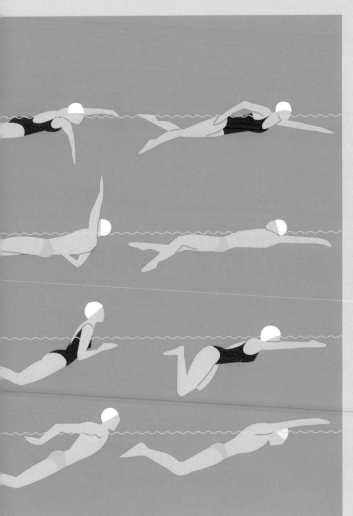

30 M BIGGEST WAVE SURFED

Surfed by Garrett McNamara in January 2013. That is the height of five giraffes or more than six double-decker buses.

FARTHEST DISTANCE JUMPED WATERSKIING

BY FREDDY KRUEGER (USA) 2008,
MORE THAN 2.5 TIMES THE LENGTH
OF A BASKETBALL COURT.

RACKET SPORTS

With projectiles rocketing towards them at the speed of a racing car, players need quick reflexes, agility, good hand-to-eye coordination and plenty of power to succeed.

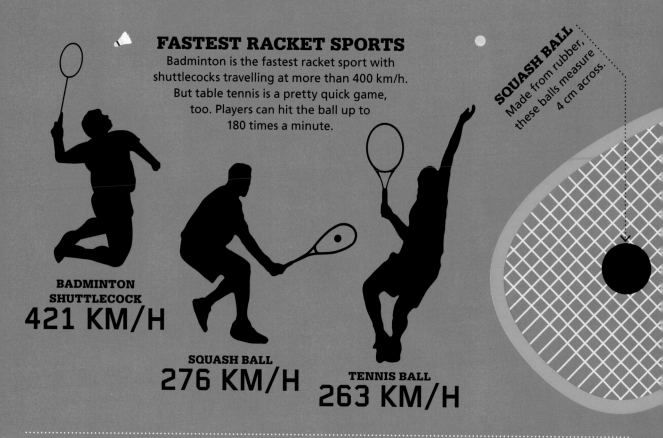

FASTEST RACKET SPORTS

Badminton is the fastest racket sport with shuttlecocks travelling at more than 400 km/h. But table tennis is a pretty quick game, too. Players can hit the ball up to 180 times a minute.

SQUASH BALL
Made from rubber, these balls measure 4 cm across.

BADMINTON SHUTTLECOCK
421 KM/H

SQUASH BALL
276 KM/H

TENNIS BALL
263 KM/H

LONGEST PROFESSIONAL TENNIS MATCH

WIMBLEDON 2011

JOHN ISNER (USA) **VS** **NICOLAS MAHUT** (FRANCE)

It lasted for 11 hours, 5 minutes, spread out over three days. They played a total of 183 games and the final set was won by Isner, 70 games to 68.

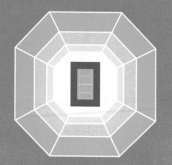

BIGGEST TENNIS ARENAS

ARTHUR ASHE STADIUM
(New York, USA)
23,200 seats

O2 ARENA
(London, UK)
17,500 seats

INDIAN WELLS TENNIS GARDEN
(California, USA)
16,100 seats

Esther Vergeer is the most successful wheelchair tennis player of all time. She was undefeated between **2003** and **2012**, winning

470 matches in a row.

EQUIPMENT

Rackets and bats come in different shapes and sizes, but all have a thin handle and a large head. Modern rackets are made of high-tech materials, such as carbon fibre, making them light, but also very strong.

SQUASH RACKET

TENNIS BALL
Made from rubber that is covered with felt, tennis balls should be no more that 6.85 cm across.

TENNIS RACKET

BADMINTON RACKET

SHUTTLECOCK
A shuttlecock has a nose made from cork that is covered with leather. Fixed to this are 16 feathers.

TABLE TENNIS BAT

TABLE TENNIS BALL
Made from lightweight plastic, a table tennis ball measures 4 cm across.

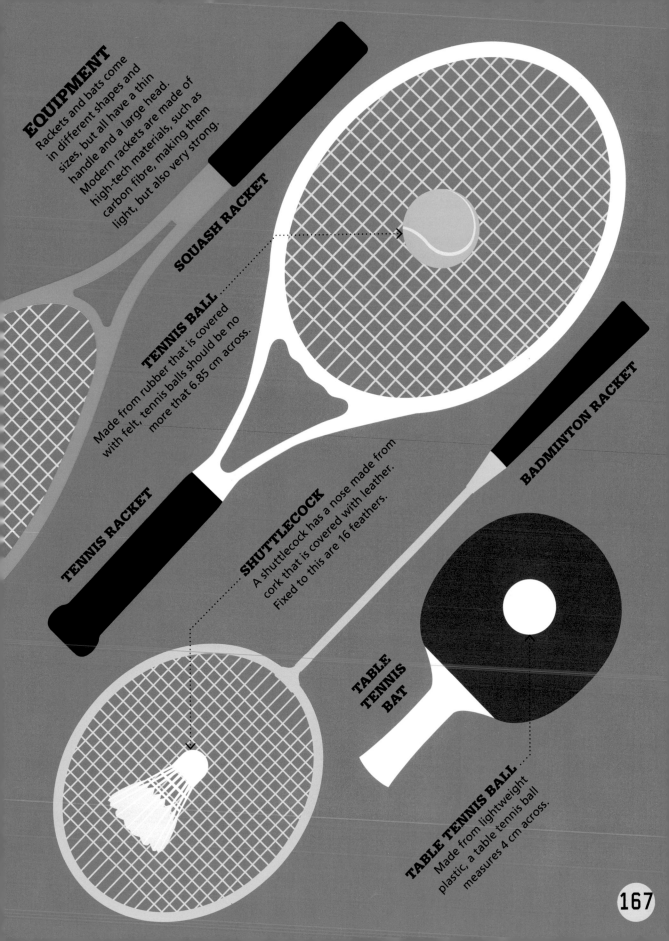

WINTER SPORTS

The cold winter months see everything from high-speed skiers hurtling downhill to snowboarders making incredible aerial leaps more than twice the height of a double-decker bus.

SPEED RECORDS

Speed skiers try to get down a slope as quickly as possible. They wear specially shaped helmets and skin-tight outfits, and use extra-long skis to help them travel faster.

SKIING MEN
251.4 KM/H
SIMONE ORIGONE
(ITALY)

NORDIC SKIING

Also known as cross-country skiing, this is one of the most physically demanding sports, using nearly 1,200 calories per hour.

SKIING WOMEN
242.6 KM/H
SANNA TIDSTRAND
(SWEDEN)

SNOWBOARDING
201.9 KM/H
DARREN POWELL
(AUSTRALIA)

9.8 M
BIGGEST AIR OUT OF A HALF-PIPE
Terje Håkonsen, Norway – 9.8 m in 2007. This is equivalent to the height of 5.5 adults.

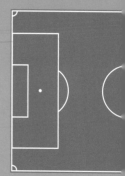

BOBSLEIGH, SKELETON AND LUGE

Individuals or teams of two or four athletes use these vehicles fitted with skates to race down an icy track.

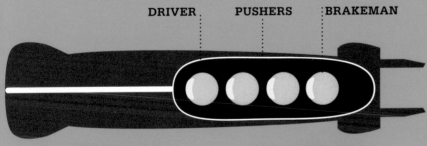

DRIVER   PUSHERS   BRAKEMAN

BOBSLEIGH
These come in two different sizes, for teams of two or four. Athletes start by pushing the bobsleigh along the track, before jumping in.

FASTEST SPEED IN A BOBSLEIGH
143 KM/H

TOP SPEED ON A SKELETON
146.4 KM/H

SKELETON
To start, the athlete runs along the track before leaping, face down, onto the skeleton.

LUGE
To start, the athlete sits on the luge before pulling themselves forwards with his or her hands and racing down the track.

TOP SPEED ON A LUGE
139.4 KM/H

246.5 M

SKI JUMPING
The longest ski jump is 246.5 metres by Johan Remen Evensen of Norway in 2011 – the length of nearly 2.5 football pitches.

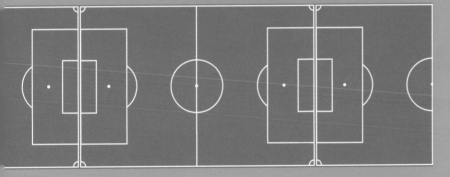

SKATING
Skaters use different types and shapes of skate, depending on the sport they are taking part in.

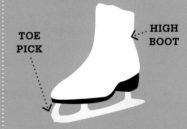

TOE PICK   HIGH BOOT

FIGURE SKATE
These have a curved blade and a toe pick, which is used for jumps and other dance moves on the ice.

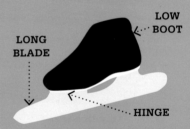

LONG BLADE   LOW BOOT   HINGE

SPEED SKATE
The blade is connected to the boot by a hinge. They are also called clap skates, because of the sound they make while skating.

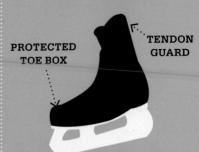

PROTECTED TOE BOX   TENDON GUARD

ICE HOCKEY SKATE
These have flat blades and a boot that is made from moulded plastic to protect and support the feet and ankles.

TARGET SPORTS

A good aim is the name of the game here, and for that target sports men and women need eyes like hawks, steady hands and a calm, focused attitude.

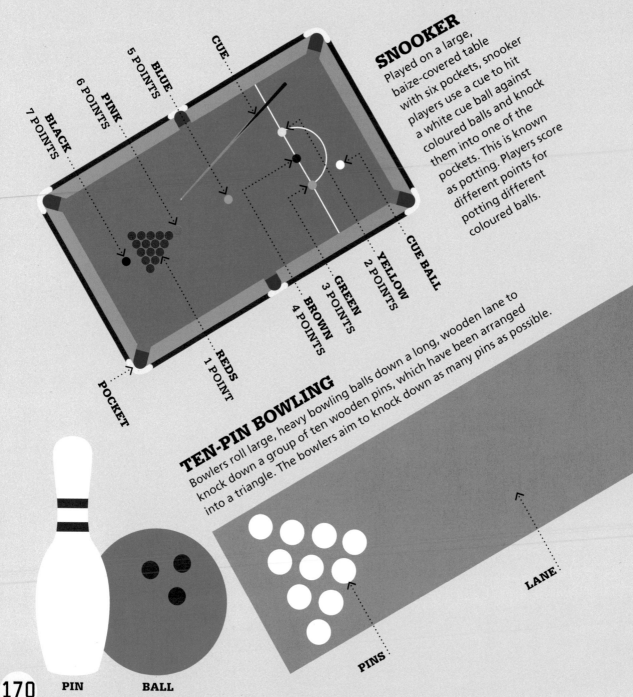

CUE

BLUE
5 POINTS

PINK
6 POINTS

BLACK
7 POINTS

SNOOKER
Played on a large, baize-covered table with six pockets, snooker players use a cue to hit a white cue ball against coloured balls and knock them into one of the pockets. This is known as potting. Players score different points for potting different coloured balls.

CUE BALL

YELLOW
2 POINTS

GREEN
3 POINTS

BROWN
4 POINTS

REDS
1 POINT

POCKET

TEN-PIN BOWLING
Bowlers roll large, heavy bowling balls down a long, wooden lane to knock down a group of ten wooden pins, which have been arranged into a triangle. The bowlers aim to knock down as many pins as possible.

LANE

PINS

PIN   **BALL**

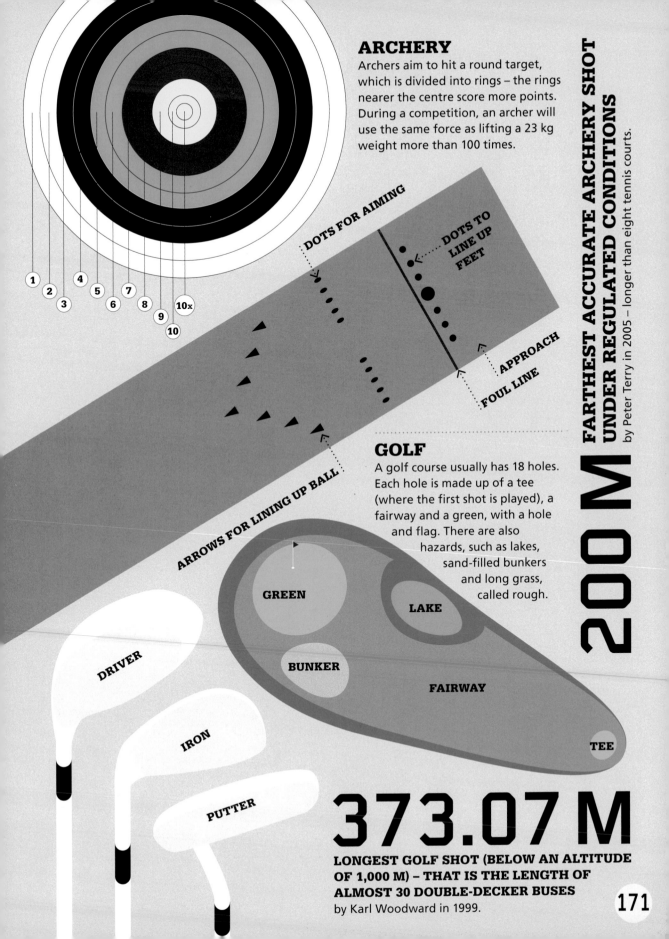

ARCHERY

Archers aim to hit a round target, which is divided into rings – the rings nearer the centre score more points. During a competition, an archer will use the same force as lifting a 23 kg weight more than 100 times.

1 2 3 4 5 6 7 8 9 10 10x

DOTS FOR AIMING

DOTS TO LINE UP FEET

APPROACH

FOUL LINE

ARROWS FOR LINING UP BALL

GOLF

A golf course usually has 18 holes. Each hole is made up of a tee (where the first shot is played), a fairway and a green, with a hole and flag. There are also hazards, such as lakes, sand-filled bunkers and long grass, called rough.

GREEN

LAKE

BUNKER

FAIRWAY

TEE

DRIVER

IRON

PUTTER

200 M
FARTHEST ACCURATE ARCHERY SHOT UNDER REGULATED CONDITIONS
by Peter Terry in 2005 – longer than eight tennis courts.

373.07 M
LONGEST GOLF SHOT (BELOW AN ALTITUDE OF 1,000 M) – THAT IS THE LENGTH OF ALMOST 30 DOUBLE-DECKER BUSES
by Karl Woodward in 1999.

171

ANIMAL SPORTS

With the fastest greyhounds capable of running nearly twice as quickly as the quickest human, it seems that sometimes four legs really are better than two.

IN JANUARY 2012, A SINGLE DUTCH RACING PIGEON WAS SOLD AT AUCTION TO A CHINESE BUYER FOR A RECORD

£209,000

HORSE RACING

Perhaps the most famous steeplechase (race over fences) is the Grand National, held at Aintree, UK. Horses and riders race over 7,242 metres and jump about 30 fences. One of the most difficult is Becher's Brook, where the landing area is much lower than the fence.

1.47 METRES

2.07 METRES

BECHER'S BROOK

OVER SHORT RACES (UP TO 160 KM), PIGEONS HAVE BEEN RECORDED FLYING AT SPEEDS OF NEARLY

180 KM/H

MAKING THEM THE FASTEST ANIMALS USED IN SPORT.

Some pigeon races are held over distances of up to 1,800 km – the equivalent of flying from London to Tangier, Morocco.

Endurance horse races cover about **160 km** and may take riders up to **12 hours** to complete.

POLO

This team sport sees groups of riders try to knock a ball through an opponent's goal using a long stick while riding an animal. It is usually played on horseback, but versions of the sport use camels and even elephants.

70.76 KM/H

The record race speed for a horse was 70.76 km/h. This was set by Winning Brew at the Penn National Race Course, Grantville, USA, in 2008.

FASTEST SPEED
FOR A GREYHOUND
72 KM/H

FASTEST SPEED
FOR A HUMAN
37.5 KM/H

CROWDS AND ARENAS

Sports can be staged almost anywhere. While many are held in specially built stadiums and arenas, some, such as the Tour de France, take place along the roads of entire countries!

SEATING

FINISH LINE

Used for chariot racing, the U-shaped Circus Maximus in ancient Rome could seat a crowd of up to

250,000

STARTING GATES

LARGEST CROWDS

The biggest games attract the biggest crowds. The world's largest sporting venue, the Indianapolis Motor Speedway, has seating for 257,325. Including standing spectators, it may be able to accommodate up to 400,000 people.

FOOTBALL
BRAZIL V
PARAGUAY 1954
MARACANÃ STADIUM, BRAZIL
183,513

BASEBALL
LA DODGERS V
BOSTON RED SOX 2008
LOS ANGELES COLISEUM, USA
115,300

ATTENDANCE FIGURES FOR CROWDS WATCHING THE ENTIRE TOUR DE FRANCE RANGE FROM **12–15** MILLION

LARGEST TEAM SPORTS ARENAS TODAY

1. RUNGRADO MAY DAY STADIUM,
PYONGYANG, NORTH KOREA

150,000

2. SALT LAKE STADIUM,
KOLKATA, INDIA
120,000

3. MICHIGAN STADIUM,
ANN ARBOR, USA
109,901

4. BEAVER STADIUM,
PENNSYLVANIA, USA
106,572

5. ESTADIO AZTECA,
MEXICO CITY, MEXICO
105,064

WEMBLEY STADIUM

Wembley Stadium, London, was built using **23,000 tonnes** of steel. The large arch used **1,750 tonnes** of steel alone, the same mass as 10 jumbo jets.

RUGBY UNION
NEW ZEALAND V AUSTRALIA 2000
STADIUM AUSTRALIA, AUSTRALIA
109,874

BASKETBALL
NBA ALL-STAR GAME 2010
COWBOYS STADIUM, USA
108,713

TENNIS
KIM CLIJSTERS (BELGIUM) V SERENA WILLIAMS (USA) 2010
KING BAUDOUIN STADIUM, BELGIUM
35,681

PRIZES AND TROPHIES

Winners of sporting competitions are usually awarded prizes. These can be cups, medals, enormous trophies and even items of clothing.

THE BIGGEST TROPHIES

DAVIS CUP
(TENNIS)
110 CM TALL
107 CM IN
DIAMETER
WEIGHS **105 KG**

STANLEY CUP
(ICE HOCKEY)
89.54 CM TALL
WEIGHS **15.5 KG**

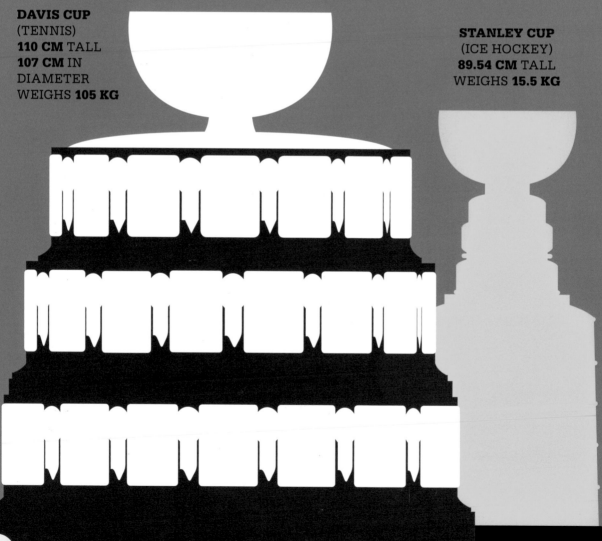

CYCLING JERSEYS

Leading riders in cycling races wear specially coloured jerseys to show which part of the race they are winning.

| RACE LEADER | LEADER OF THE POINTS CLASSIFICATION | KING OF THE MOUNTAINS | BEST YOUNG RIDER | CURRENT WORLD CHAMPION |

OLYMPIC MEDALS

Winning athletes at the Olympics and Paralympics are awarded gold medals. However, very little of the medal is actually gold, with most of it being made from silver and copper.

GOLD MEDALS
92.5% silver, 6.16% copper, 1.34% gold

SILVER MEDALS
92.5% silver, 7.5% copper

BRONZE MEDALS
97% copper, 2.5% zinc 0.5% tin

FOOTBALL WORLD CUP
36 CM TALL

VINCE LOMBARDI TROPHY
(AMERICAN FOOTBALL)
56 CM TALL

WEBB ELLIS CUP
(RUGBY UNION)
38 CM TALL

Winners of golf's Masters Tournament are awarded a green jacket.

THE ASHES URN

England and Australia take part in the Ashes, a series of five-day cricket test matches. The winners are given a replica of a small, 10-cm-tall urn, the original of which is said to hold the ashes of a burnt cricket bail.

GLOSSARY

Absolute zero
The coldest possible temperature, -273.15°C, at which point molecules stop moving completely.

Aerofoil
The special shape of a wing, which produces higher pressure below than above, creating a pushing force. This force can lift an aircraft into the air or push a racing car down into the track to improve its grip.

Air mail
Letters, parcels and other mail that is delivered by air, usually between different countries.

Agglomeration
A continuous built-up area, which may be made up of several towns and cities that are joined by suburbs and other urban areas.

Atlas
A collection of maps in a book.

Attract
When an object pulls something towards itself. Opposite magnetic poles on two magnets will be attracted to each other.

Biennial
Happening every two years; an event that happens twice a year is biannual.

Bobsleigh
A winter sport where two or four athletes at a time race down an ice track while sitting in a bobsleigh.

Broadcast
The transmission of a TV or radio programme to the public.

Buoyancy
The ability of a ship or boat to float in water. A ship will float if it weighs less than the same volume of water.

Byte
A unit of computer information made up of 8 bits. There are 1,024 bytes in a kilobyte, 1,024 kilobytes in a megabyte, 1,024 megabytes in a gigabyte and 1,024 gigabytes in a terabyte.

Canopy
The layer of interconnecting treetops in a rainforest, high above the forest floor, but just below the emergents.

Canyon
A type of gorge or chasm with very steep sides cut into the landscape by flowing water – usually a river.

Language
A common form of speech and writing shared by a people, usually living in the same country.

Cellular network
A set of radio transmitters and receivers used to send information, such as telephone calls. The network is divided into units called cells, each of which has its own antenna.

Ceramics
Objects made from soft clay, which are then heated to a high temperature in order to make them hard.

Clean and jerk
A weight-lifting discipline where the athlete tries to lift the weight above his or her head in two movements.

Comic strip
A short story told in a series of cartoon pictures, often printed in newspapers.

Composted
When biodegradable materials, such as waste food, are allowed to rot. This produces compost which can be used to feed crops and gardens.

Compression
When something is squeezed together.

Console
A special type of computer used for playing video games.

Corporation
A very large company or group of companies.

Debt
The amount of money that is owed by a person, company or even an entire country.

Dependency
Territories that are governed by – or dependent on – other countries.

Desertification
The process by which fertile land gradually becomes infertile and turns into barren desert.

Global exposure
The amount of the world where a company operates and employs people.

Diamond
The diamond-shaped area around which a baseball game is played.

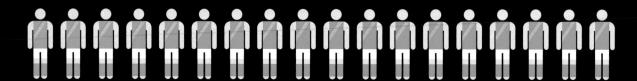

Diphtheria

A disease spread by bacteria that causes coughing and breathing difficulties. It also causes death in around 10 per cent of sufferers.

Dual-flush toilet

A toilet that has two types of flush: a small flush for liquid waste; and a large flush for solid waste.

E-book

A book that is read on an electronic device known as an e-reader.

Emergent

The highest trees in a rainforest that 'emerge' from the top of the canopy.

Emissions

Gases and chemicals that are produced by motor vehicle engines, factories and power plants. These emissions are expelled into the air through exhausts and chimneys.

Energy-saving light bulb

A type of light bulb that uses just 10 per cent of the energy and lasts 10 times longer than an incandescent light bulb.

Equator

An imaginary line running horizontally around the centre of the Earth. It is the line of 0° latitude.

Folio

A book made of sheets of paper that have been folded in the middle.

Fulcrum

The point around which a lever works. It is also known as the pivot.

Friction

The force produced when two objects or materials rub together.

director

The person in charge of making a movie, who tells the actors and crew what they have to do.

Rough objects produce more friction, making them harder to move, while smooth objects produce less friction.

GDP
Gross domestic product – the total value of all the goods and services produced by a nation.

Gears
Wheels or bars with teeth that interlock with the teeth on other wheels or a chain. They are used to transmit a force.

Geothermal
Relating to heat created beneath the Earth's surface. Geothermal energy can be used to heat water to produce steam and produce electricity.

Gigawatt hours
A large unit of energy – the amount of power (in gigawatts, the equivalent of 1,000 megawatts or 1 billion watts) produced every hour.

Glacier
A thick body of ice that moves very slowly down a mountain valley.

Global warming
An increase in the average temperature of the Earth's atmosphere, which may be caused by man-made pollution.

Greenhouse gases
Gases such as carbon dioxide and methane that trap the Sun's energy in the Earth's atmosphere and heat it up. This is similar to how the glass of a greenhouse traps the heat within.

incandescent light bulb
A type of brightly shining electric light bulb.

Gross national income
The total value of goods and services produced by a nation (the Gross Domestic Product), plus any revenue received from foreign countries, minus any payments made to foreign countries.

Half-pipe
A U-shaped channel carved through the snow. Skiers and snowboarders can use the sides of the channel to perform jumps and tricks.

HD-TV
High-definition television – a type of TV that shows images in great detail.

Highest-grossing
Something that has made the most amount of money. Gross is the total amount of money earned by selling something before deductions (the amount of money spent on making the item). The total gross minus the deductions is the profit.

steeplechase
A form of horse racing where the horses and riders race over a course with jumps and fences.

Hydraulics

A system that uses a liquid to transmit a force. Squeezing the liquid at one end will produce a pushing force at the other end of the system. The size of the force can be adjusted by altering the size of the cylinders and pistons.

Tectonic plates
The enormous sheets of rock that make up the Earth's surface.

Hydroelectric dam

A large dam built across a river, which uses the controlled flow of water through the dam to produce electricity.

Hydroelectric power station

A power station that uses the movement of water to produce electricity. This water is usually stored in a large, artificial lake.

Incinerated

When something is destroyed by burning it.

Internal combustion

The process of producing a driving force by burning a fuel inside a cylinder. This explosion pushes a piston down and this motion can be used to move a vehicle or power machinery.

International Date Line

An imaginary line running through the Pacific Ocean from the North Pole to the South Pole. The date changes by one day either side of the line. It is the line of 180° longitude.

Jet

A type of engine that sucks in air and burns fuel to create a powerful jet of hot gases that roars out of the back of the engine, pushing the jet forwards.

Knot

A unit of speed used to measure the movement of ships and boats. It stands for 'nautical miles per hour'.

Landfill

A large hole in the ground into which waste and rubbish are dumped and then covered over.

Landlocked

A country that does not have a border with the sea, but is surrounded on all sides by other countries.

Lever

A long bar that moves around a pivot, or fulcrum, to transmit a force. Levers are usually used to move or lift an object.

Walk of Fame
A pavement in Hollywood, USA, where the names of famous movie stars have been engraved in stars.

Library
A collection of reading and artistic materials, such as books, newspapers and records. Libraries can often be visited by people who want to study or borrow the materials.

Life expectancy
The average age to which a person can expect to live.

Luge
A type of winter sport where athletes race down an ice track while lying face-up on a luge sled.

Mandatory
Something that has to happen. Mandatory holidays are days off that companies have to give their workers.

Marathon
A long-distance running race, where athletes compete to see who can finish a 42-km route the quickest. It is usually held on the streets of a city, rather than inside an arena.

Market value
The total value of a company. This is decided by the value of the company's shares as they are bought and sold at stock markets in various parts of the world.

Morse code
An alphabet that uses a system of dots and dashes to represent letters. Morse code signals can be sent using a light or as pulses along electric wires.

Nordic skiing
A form of skiing where people propel themselves along using poles and skis, rather than skiing down a mountain slope.

Novel
A fictional story mostly printed in book form. Graphic novels tell stories using pictures and words.

Olympics
A major sporting event held every four years for both summer and winter sports. Athletes from all over the world gather in a host city to take part.

Opera
A drama where the actors sing to music played by an orchestra. An opera is also a building where theatrical performances are staged.

Orchestra
A large group of musicians who play various instruments including strings, woodwinds, brass and percussion.

Paralympics
A major sporting event held every four years for athletes with physical disabilities and learning difficulties. It is held just after the Summer and Winter Olympics.

Payload
The cargo carried by an aircraft or rocket, which earns money. A rocket's payload can include a satellite, a space probe or a fee-paying astronaut.

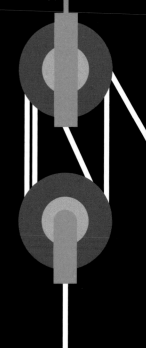

Pulley
A simple machine that uses a system of ropes and wheels to move an object. The more times the rope passes through the system, the easier it is to move the object.

Pins

Ten wooden objects that are used as targets in ten-pin bowling. They are arranged in a triangle at the end of a bowling lane for bowlers to aim at.

Pixel

Short for 'picture elements', pixels are the dots that make up images on computer screens.

Pole

One of the two ends of a magnet. A magnetic pole can be either North (N) or South (S).

Pole vault

A sport in which an athlete tries to jump, or vault, over a high bar using a long, flexible pole to push up with.

Polo

A team sport where athletes ride animals or bicycles and hit a ball using long sticks in an attempt to score in the opposition goal.

Population

The people who live in a particular area, such as a country.

Population density

The number of people living in a particular area.

Prolific

Producing a lot of work – a prolific author has written a lot of books.

Public debt

The amount of money owed by a country's government.

Public holidays

Holidays that are taken to celebrate occasions that are important to a whole country or a specific group of people.

Range

The distance an object or vehicle can travel. The range of a vehicle is usually the distance it can travel without having to refuel.

Repel

When an object pushes something away from itself. If two magnetic poles that are the same are put close to each other, they will repel and push each other away.

Locomotive

The powered vehicle that is used to move a train. Locomotives can be driven by steam, internal combustion engines, electric motors or magnets.

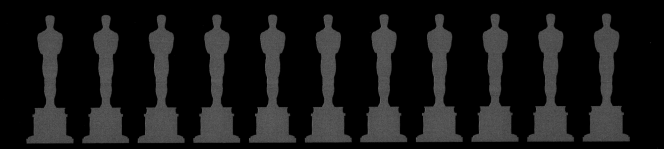

Republic

A country that is ruled by a president rather than a monarch. The president is usually voted for by the people of the country.

Resources

Materials that can be used to produce goods or energy. These can include natural resources, such as coal, oil and minerals, and human resources, such as the size of a workforce.

Return

The amount of money made by selling something.

River basin

The area of land that feeds a river and its tributaries (small rivers that flow into the main river) with water.

Rocket

A type of engine that carries both fuel and oxygen in solid or liquid form. These are mixed and burned to produce hot gases that push the rocket forwards.

Satellite

A spacecraft launched into orbit around the Earth.

Shares

A small proportion of a company which can be bought or sold by people or other companies. The total worth of a company's shares decides the company's market value.

Shuttlecock

The projectile used in badminton. It consists of a rubber nose with feathers attached to the back to make it fly correctly.

Silicon

A material on which tiny marks can be made using a laser. These marks can hold a lot of information, which is why silicon is used to make computers and other electronic devices.

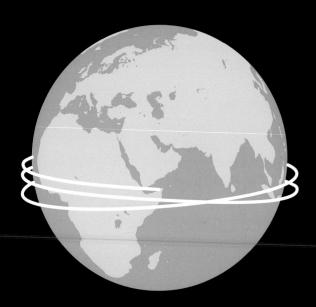

Skeleton

In this fast winter sport, athletes race down an ice track while lying face-down on a skeleton sled.

Snatch
A weight-lifting discipline where the athlete tries to lift the weight above his or her head in one movement.

Soap opera
A long-running TV series featuring one set of characters.

Solar panel
A panel that converts light energy from the Sun into electricity.

Stadium
A large building in which sporting events are held. The largest stadiums can hold more than 100,000 people.

Stock exchange
A place where company shares and other economic products are bought and sold.

Streamlined
An object that is streamlined is able to move through the air or through water as easily as possible.

Superstition
A belief that doing something will somehow affect something else, even if the two things seem unrelated.

Tablet
A small computer device that just has a screen and no keyboard. Instructions are typed directly onto the screen, which is touch-sensitive.

Top fuel
The fastest and most-powerful form of dragster racing.

Trade
The buying and selling of goods between different peoples, regions and countries.

Trophy
A prize given to the winners, or highest placed athletes, in a sporting competition.

Turbine
A large bladed wheel that is sent spinning as water or wind moves past it.

fairway
The corridor of short grass along a golf hole, which leads from the tee area to the green.